STORYTELLING

IN FILM AND

TELEVISION

STORYTELLING IN FILM AND TELEVISION

Kristin Thompson

Harvard University Press

Cambridge, Massachusetts, and London, England   *2003*

Library of Congress Cataloging-in-Publication Data
Thompson, Kristin, 1950–
    Storytelling in film and television / Kristin Thompson.
        p. cm.
    Includes bibliographical references and index.
    ISBN 0-674-01063-9 (cloth : alk. paper) —
    ISBN 0-674-01087-6 (paperback : alk. paper)
        1. Television authorship.   2. Motion picture authorship.   I. Title.
 ⌣ PN1992.7 .T47 2003
    808'.066791—dc21   2002192204

For Dr. Marilyn Butler and Sir John Hanson,
with thanks for two wonderful weeks in Oxford

CONTENTS

PREFACE

Popular films and television series tell stories in an entertaining, easily comprehensible fashion. They seem simple, yet often the audience must keep track of several characters, multiple plot lines, motifs, and thematic meanings. Television viewers often face the additional challenge of frequent interruptions—for commercials, for week-long gaps between episodes, and even for stretches of time between seasons. Yet they manage, remarkably, to keep track of not only a single long-running narrative, but often several simultaneously. How do film and television writers juggle the need for graspable, enjoyable stories with the many restrictions imposed by their respective commercial formats? How do those two art forms differ in the ways they tell stories? Such questions are not often asked by scholars of film and television, yet they seem crucial to a thorough understanding of how television programs are created and how they affect their viewers.

In early 2001, I was given the opportunity to explore these and other questions. I received an invitation to visit Oxford University as the News International Visiting Professor of Broadcast Media. This two-week visit, under the joint auspices of Exeter and Green

Colleges, involved four lectures on various formal similarities and differences between the storytelling tactics of film and television.

As I prepared these lectures, one trait of mainstream television narrative became increasingly clear. Because television programs typically face far greater restrictions of time and format than films, the storytelling tactics of television often appear extremely simple, especially in situation comedies and dramas with only one or two plotlines. Since the 1980s, dramas with multiple storylines have been praised as introducing complexity into narrative television. I shall argue, however, that good situation comedies and "simple" dramas often in fact also have an underlying complexity. Indeed, many of the interesting aspects of storytelling are hidden in television in a way that they are not in most other arts. We watch television via single episodes, and those episodes may be unremarkable. Yet television is structured in ways that become apparent only if we take the long view. Multiple-episode programs structure narratives within episodes, across seasons, and across a potentially lengthy succession of seasons.

To some extent, both classical films and television programs hide their own cleverness in a show of simplicity. In television particularly, the complexity fades into the tenuous connections across a series. Similarly, the virtues of the individual episode—compact exposition, swift progression from cause to effect, establishment of material for future entries in the series—make little impression unless one pays keen attention or undertakes actual analysis, either of the episode or across the season.

My first chapter tackles the issue of how one might do that sort of close narrative analysis within episodes. I begin by considering a concept that has been prominent in the history of television studies and that has, it seems to me, discouraged such close analysis: Raymond Williams's notion of "flow." I then address the matter of what narrative techniques film and television share. These include the interweaving of two (or more) plotlines, the use of clear temporal indicators like appointments and deadlines, establishing tactics placed early in scenes, and the insertion of "dangling causes" to stitch temporally separated scenes together. Such analytical concepts, which have already been applied to film, can be applied as well to the younger art form.

Film and television are, however, two different (if overlapping) media. I am concerned here not with the technical and stylistic contrasts between them but rather with the ways in which they have been used to tell stories. Historically, they have developed largely distinctive formats. Most particularly, feature films tend to be longer than most television programs; they are typically watched individually as self-contained stories. Television programs, however, may cluster into a temporal unit for viewers, with interruptions at intervals; many series tell stories serially. Thus the artistic possibilities for storytelling that the two formats offer also differ significantly. The second chapter changes direction to focus on some of those differences. These arise from the constraints that exist in television, to do partly with restricted time spans for individual episodes and partly with the inevitable interruptions within and between episodes. I argue that teleplay writers have developed a set of particular narrative tactics to deal with these restraints. I begin by examining what practitioners have advised in the how-to writing manuals on television scripts, then go on to suggest other tactics that are less explicitly practiced by writers. The similarities and differences in conventions for endings and narrative closure in film and television are particularly important, and I reserve dealing with those for the third chapter.

Film production and television production have long been symbiotically linked. The same company may produce both mov-

ies and TV programs. Films have been a staple part of the television schedule since the early 1960s, and adaptations between the
two media are increasingly common. The third chapter explores
the enormously expanded demand for narrative material generated by the mass media in the late twentieth and early twenty-first
centuries and its implication for the nature of narrative. Adaptations, serials, and sequels have, I suggest, loosened traditional
notions of closure and the ties between narrative and individual
author—a process that has influenced literature as well as the
emerging electronic media (for example, Internet-based systems
like massively multiplayer online role-playing games). Thus television has, whether one likes it or not, had a major impact on the
arts in general.

Having concentrated on mainstream popular television, I
branch out in the fourth chapter to consider the notion of
whether there might be an "art television." The phrase derives
from a familiar and established phrase in film studies, the "art cinema." Do programs comparable to art films ever get made and
shown on broadcast television? One obvious candidate for such a
designation would be David Lynch's *Twin Peaks*, which has often
been juxtaposed with his art film *Blue Velvet*. I examine some of
the traits often ascribed to art films and find parallel examples in
these two works by Lynch, as well as in a number of other candidates for "art television" status.

These four chapters do not offer a comprehensive overview of
this large topic. Rather, they are meant as essayistic investigations
of four intertwined issues. Hence I have not attempted to recast
the original lectures extensively. Instead, I have made minor revi-
sions in response to some of the points made in the discussion periods after each lecture. Some of my examples were drawn from
current series, and I have updated the information in relation to

them. I have also added some references to relevant sources, indicating how the issues I raise here might be followed up. Indeed, I hope that the ideas I raise here may suggest possibilities for one type of research that might usefully be added to the growing field of television studies.

I would like to thank the heads of the two host colleges, Sir John Hanson, Warden of Green College, and Dr. Marilyn Butler, Rector of Exeter College, for their enthusiastic support during the arrangements for the lectures themselves and for their generous hospitality during my stay in Oxford. David Butler proved the ideal co-host at Exeter. Kay Honner, Erica Sheppard, and Paul Burns handled many of the logistical aspects of the visit, including making the lectures run smoothly despite my need for a variety of visual aids. Thanks also to Anthony Smith of Magdalen College for his support.

Here at the University of Wisconsin–Madison, Paddy Rourke and the staff of the media center of the Dept. of Communication Arts have been most cooperative. I am particularly grateful to Julie D'Acci, of the same department, who lent unstintingly of both her encouragement and her considerable expertise in television studies during the preparation of these lectures. Thanks also to David Bordwell, who not only gave his usual cogent editorial advice but also spent a long evening helping me dub my video clips from NTSC to Pal.

STORYTELLING

IN FILM AND

TELEVISION

GO WITH THE FLOW?

ANALYZING TELEVISION

NARRATIVE IN TWO MEDIA

Television is not a poor cousin of film that cannot be studied on its own. Quite the contrary, film and television studies, though often linked within individual institutions, have grown up in parallel as two separate disciplines. Each field has its own history and its own body of material for study. As of now they are two distinct media, or art forms if you prefer. Yet technological developments are currently bringing them closer together, what with digital video rapidly improving and satellite-based projection systems already being tried out in a few cinemas. Perhaps someday film and television will be largely indistinguishable, converging into a single "moving-image" medium. In the meantime, however, they certainly share the ability to tell stories with moving images, using photography, editing, staging, and so on. These common technical means offer some of the same possibilities and limitations to both media.

Before proceeding, we might ask: How can we undertake a critical analysis of television narrative? Television studies are hardly well enough established that the desirability of such analysis will be apparent to everyone. I shall be assuming here that television is an art form, parallel to the older, more familiar art forms. I do not use the term "art" qualitatively here, as in, "That painting is awful. I don't call *that* art." Instead, I assume simply that any medium produces both bad art and good art. You may be of the opinion that television has produced few if any masterpieces, but after all, the vast majority of works created in any medium are not masterpieces and are soon forgotten.

When I was originally preparing my lecture series, I told a friend here in England that I would be talking about television at Oxford. She claimed that she almost never watched television, implying that it was not worthwhile. Yet when I added that I was thinking about using *Yes, Minister* as an example, my friend brightened up and began to praise the intelligent writing and the humor of that series. Most people, I suspect, can think of at least some television programs they have enjoyed for similar reasons.

In this book, I emphasize examples from well-regarded, popular programs. I have done this not because I intend to offer you a "Masterpieces of Television" approach, but rather because I want to look at programs that might be considered normative in their uses of narrative technique—the sorts of programs an aspiring screenwriter might be given as models of how television should be done. In these kinds of programs, I believe, the techniques are most clearly to be discerned.

In seeking programs to analyze, I necessarily limited my focus. My purpose is to examine narrative fiction series, made in English and specifically in the United States and Britain. I concentrate primarily on the short forms of television, which consist most commonly of the half-hour situation comedy and the one-hour drama. Narratives in such programs seem to me to offer the most noteworthy differences from feature films. I do not intend to look at the social impact of these programs, their ideological content, or their production background. Such approaches are well represented in television studies already. Aesthetic analysis, however, is not, and it is quite a large enough area to tackle in this book.

FLOW OR INTERRUPTION?

Why have television programs so seldom been studied from an aesthetic perspective? Indeed, why have they so seldom been treated as entertainment rather than as evidence of some aspect—usually negative—of modern society? I need briefly to deal with these questions, since there are assumptions commonly circulating within television studies that would tend to discourage treating television programs—and especially individual episodes of television series—aesthetically.

There seem to be at least three general reasons for this dearth of close analysis. Some hold a lingering prejudice against taking television seriously as an art form. Alternatively, some scholars would subsume individual programs into the broader field of cultural production, encompassing many media. And third, many scholars have relied—extensively, I shall suggest—on the televisual "flow," or overall scheduling, rather than on single programs.

In the early decades of television, theorists and critics working in the more established arts were reluctant to scrutinize the new medium closely. Given that a major portion of television has consisted of narratives presented in moving images and sound, we might expect analytical methods from literature and from film studies to provide useful starting points for studying it. Yet experts in those areas seldom applied their methods to television.

Scholars of literature tended to dismiss television or to consider it an actual threat to cultural standards and to education. Television historian John Hartley has described the effects of this bias for the budding field of television studies:

> The textual tradition in British TV studies began when people trained in literary theory and "practical criticism" turned their attention to popular culture. Unfortunately for the cause of television analysis, such training tended to emphasize strong hostility to popular cultural aesthetics, and fear of the cultural impact of new entertainment media. So whereas many traditions of study in the general area of the arts have presumed some pleasurable investment by the student in the object of study, the textual tradition in television studies set out with the avowed intention of denouncing television and all its works. People who specialize in the textual study of forms like literature, the visual arts, photography or even cinema are presumed either to *like* their chosen form, or to have some talent in its textual *creation*. But the opposite was true of TV studies when it entered the academy; the successful student was one who could catalogue most extensively the supposed evils associated with television.[1]

Certainly in the late 1960s and the 1970s, during which period I entered graduate school, the field of film studies was struggling to establish itself within the academy and to argue convincingly for film as a distinctive art form. A close link to television could have been seen as holding film studies back in these enterprises.

A second reason for the dearth of attention paid to individual programs is that the few aesthetic analyses of television that did appear were based on assumptions that were rapidly being pushed into obscurity by new trends within academia. Critics who chose prestigious individual programs to analyze often did so on the basis of the originality and excellence of their scripts: for instance, *The Singing Detective* and *Yes, Minister*.[2] By the 1970s, however, areas like film and literary studies were experiencing a shift toward the more general field of cultural studies. Here artworks were to be treated not as masterpieces by great artists but symptomatically in terms of their reflections of modern society.[3]

One of the most prominent scholars of television, Horace Newcomb, dismisses the formal analysis of the medium in this way:

> The television "critic" . . . often basing his work on the analysis of literature or film, succeeds in calling attention to the distinctive qualities of the medium, to the special nature of television fiction. But this approach all too often ignores important questions of production and reception. Intent on correcting what it takes to be a skewed interest in such matters, it often avoids the "business" of television and its "technology."[4]

This attitude falls into the "but-you-didn't-do-x syndrome" so common in both film and television studies—as if limiting one's topic were somehow a fault. To me, succeeding in "calling attention to the distinctive qualities of the medium, to the special nature of television fiction" sounds like a major accomplishment. Indeed, I would be happy in a modest way to contribute to that endeavor through this book. Other spheres of culture, even those directly related to the institution of television as a whole, may be simply irrelevant to the topic the analyst defines.

A third impediment to examining the artistic strategies of programs is a concept that has been prominent in television studies for the past twenty-five years. That concept is termed *flow*, and it is often closely tied to cultural studies. Flow most basically means the scheduling of programs and the advertising breaks within and between them considered as a continuum. (The term *flow* is not actually used within the television industry.) The result is intended to keep the viewer tuned to a single station. Beyond this, the exact meaning of the term is difficult to pin down. Critics also apply *flow* to the experience of the viewer, who supposedly sees the breaks in the television schedule not as interruptions but as part of the programs.

This second idea of flow as applied to the viewer's experience was formulated in 1974 by one of the most important cultural critics to take an interest in the young medium, Raymond Williams. In his book *Television: Technology and Cultural Form*, Williams described how he conceived the idea: "One night in Miami, still dazed from a week on an Atlantic liner, I began watching a film and at first had some difficulty in adjusting to a much greater frequency of commercial 'breaks.'" Presumably more used to BBC-style noncommercial programming, he was unable to cope with the large number of advertisements typical of late-night American programming. The result, as Williams describes it, was "a very difficult experience to interpret . . . what came to seem— for all the occasional bizarre disparities—a single irresponsible flow of images and feelings." Far from dismissing this as an anomalous experience brought on by exhaustion, Williams instead took it to be emblematic of all television viewing:

> In all developed broadcasting systems the characteristic organization, and therefore the characteristic experience, is one of sequence or flow. This phenomenon, of planned flow, is

then perhaps the defining characteristic of broadcasting, simultaneously as a technology and as a cultural form.

In all communications systems before broadcasting the essential items were discrete.[5]

Williams's exact definition of flow remains difficult to determine, and later critics have interpreted it in different ways.

Please note, however, how this passage links two senses of flow: Williams assumes that "the characteristic organization" of television, that is, the scheduling, is "therefore the characteristic experience" for the viewer. Note also that Williams claims that all media before broadcasting contained "discrete" items. He ignores the fact that since at least the nineteenth century, several popular entertainment forms had juxtaposed small units, often including advertisements: serial novels, music hall shows, and fiction magazines, for instance. Similarly, for the first twenty years of the cinema, audiences attended programs of short films whose subjects and titles they did not know in advance, and some of these were advertisements. For decades after the feature film was standardized around 1915, newsreels, cartoons, and previews preceded the main attraction. Television was hardly as novel a challenge to the public as Williams's claims imply. Moreover, although several countries, including the U.K., based their broadcast systems primarily on noncommercial, public-service channels, Williams used his American-inspired notion of flow as the defining trait of the medium.

Given that one's commonsense view might be that commercials interrupt programs rather then forming part of them, one might then question exactly what Williams thought they did. In a later interview, Williams made clear his belief that commercials actually form parts of the programs. Discussing the examples of flow he had given in his book, he remarked, "Where it seemed to me to work very clearly was in the flow of miscellaneous news items, or miscellaneous news items with commercials—which I have always argued don't interrupt the programs, they help to constitute them."[6] Although here Williams speaks of news programs, he clearly intends his generalization about flow to refer to television of all sorts.

The concept of flow, though neither self-evidently useful nor true, has been immensely influential in television studies up to the present day. One historian claims that "it is safe to say that the concept of flow has been so important to the development of television criticism that the more general scope and purpose of [Williams's] book itself is barely recalled."[7]

In fact, so pervasive has the concept of flow become that television theorists often seem unable to conceive of an approach that does not rely on this root metaphor. One historian wrote recently, in discussing how viewers tend to "drift" from one program to another, "It is precisely this possible 'drifting' through an evening's viewing that has come to seem, to many commentators, one of the unique features of television watching, and hence something that must be attended to in any account of the television text."[8]

Perhaps scholars embraced the idea of flow because it provided a convenient solution to the problem they wanted to answer in order to define their new field of study: What is the specificity of the television medium? Perhaps assuming simply that television narrative derived directly from traditional drama and film, they dismissed the idea that the medium's specificity could be found by studying individual programs.

In 1984, film and television scholar Nick Browne seemed to say as much. He proposed that all the televised material ever broadcast constituted a "supertext." As a method of tackling the study of that huge, unwieldy (and constantly expanding) supertext, he advised the analysis of segments of programming as representative samples of the whole. He commented dismissively on traditional textual analysis:

> Of course, the application of received methods of textual analysis to particular programs, provided that they can be separated from the flow and can be retrieved and held for inspection, will yield a certain kind of result. Allied with generic, narrative, or even ideological analysis, the result of textual analysis of television programs can be generalized in accord with the existing models provided by literary or film study. Yet, the application of these methods or perspectives to the "television text" can only incompletely grasp its specificity of form, force, and signification.[9]

Again we see a call for an impossibly broad study of a "supertext" that would account for absolutely all its possible aspects and relations to the world. A more modest (and practicable) analysis, though it might answer certain questions quite adequately, is dismissed as not grasping the "specificity" of the "television text." Browne's call for analysis of only the "supertext" undoubtedly pushed Williams's idea to an extreme point, and his claims are not indicative of how television studies actually developed. Nevertheless, it suggests why the field might have veered away from close analysis early on.

As I have suggested, because of this faith in the flow model many scholars have been reluctant to analyze individual television programs. Instead, during the early years of television studies, some students wrote papers and theses, and some senior scholars generated articles focused on great swatches of television schedules—whether for an entire evening, a week, a month, or even longer. In some cases, isolated episodes were analyzed with their commercial breaks treated as part of the unit under consideration.

Most researchers do not question the basic validity of Williams's original notion but try to update or refine it. The most prominent attempts have centered on the role of the audience caught up in the flow of the viewing experience. Commentators have criticized Williams for treating spectators as passive recipients of whatever the programmers choose to put in front of them.[10] At times Williams's discussions of flow certainly seem to imply such passivity: "It is evident that what is now called 'an evening's viewing' is in some ways planned by providers and then by viewers, *as a whole*."[11] Of the various breaks within programs he allows that "[o]f course many people who watch television still register some of these items as 'interruptions'"[12]—a distinctly condescending formulation hinting that at best these more alert viewers can merely "register" breaks, and then only some of them.

Within the cultural-studies area, there have been attempts to analyze television with a more active viewer in mind. Most authors point out that technology has changed since Williams's day, usually in ways that encourage the spectator to control the sequence of viewing. The remote control allows viewers to move easily among networks, while cable and satellite systems have provided many viewers with a hugely expanded selection of channels. Home video and the Internet have created further alternatives to the television broadcast schedule.

One well-known response to these changes has been Horace Newcomb and Paul T. Hirsch's concept of "viewing strips," units of television created by viewers switching among channels. These they equate quite directly with Williams's original idea of flow. Newcomb and Hirsch describe their research procedures thus:

"By taping entire weeks of television content, and tracing various potential strips in the body of that week, we construct a huge range of potential 'texts' that may have been seen by individual viewers."[13] One obvious problem here is that the explosion of cable and satellite distribution systems makes taping a complete week's worth of programming virtually impossible. Beyond that, Newcomb and Hirsch can posit only what they call "potential strips" and "potential 'texts,'" none of which may actually coincide with what any real viewers watched. Given that viewers can change channels at any moment and any number of times in that week, the possibilities are indefinitely large. Why is analyzing one hypothetical viewing strip any more valid that analyzing a single program? After all, some viewers do switch on their sets to watch specific programs and switch them off at the end—especially in this era of time shifting.[14]

Another prominent cultural analyst of television, John Fiske, is more critical of Williams's view of flow. For Fiske, the viewer does not passively absorb programs in a flow. In his view: "Flow, with its connotations of a languid river, is perhaps an unfortunate metaphor: the movement of the television text is discontinuous, interrupted, and segmented. Its attempts at closure, at a unitary meaning, or a unified viewing subject, are constantly subjected to fracturing forces." Nevertheless, Fiske still conceives the object of study as greater than the individual program, since the viewer's chance for control comes in the gaps among program segments. For Fiske, "in these the viewer 'enters the text' in [an] imaginative and creative way . . . Segmentation allows another form of 'writing' by the active viewer—zapping [changing channels frequently with only brief pauses to assess what is on each one]."[15] This influential approach prefers studying the reactions of actual audience members rather than the programs they watch.[16] As Fiske's quotation suggests, it also denies the usefulness of analyzing individual narratives, since the impossibility of closure would presumably render individual episodes of programs virtually irrelevant.

I would like to take a different tack and suggest that flow does not even capture the experience of a viewer who avoids zapping. (Indeed, it is hard to imagine a viewer spending a large portion of an evening zapping and never settling to watch anything.) Flow was from the start a misleading concept, one which had a much more limited potential for television studies than Williams and many subsequent scholars have believed.

Flow undoubtedly does, however, describe the effect that TV executives *hope* will result from their scheduling—though again, these executives seldom if ever use the term *flow* itself. Their main consideration is to keep people tuned to their channel for the entire time that the television is on, and no doubt flow would be a useful concept for a scholar studying programming as such. Todd Gitlin's book *Inside Prime Time* uses the term *flow* much as Williams intended it in its most basic sense:

> Producers produce programs, and development executives advocate them, but the top executives as a group compose schedules. Scheduling meetings dwell not only on the demographics expected but on problems of "flow": would an eight-o'clock audience of given demographics stay tuned to show X at eight-thirty, given the competition?[17]

As this passage suggests, demographics and flow are intimately related in programming. Clearly programmers would not want to create flow in the Raymond Williams sense. If viewers could not tell the advertisements from the programs' narratives, how would they know they are supposed to buy something?[18]

In the U.S. we are especially familiar with the practice of new programs being scheduled directly after established ones in the hopes that people will stayed tuned and become fans of the new show. There are terms for this strategic placement of new or failing shows: *lead-in* for the strong show, *hammocking* for a weak show placed between two strong ones, *tentpoling* for an alternation of strong and weak shows. More recently, networks have sometimes simply thrown a group of strong shows into a single evening to try and assure dominance of at least one or two nights' ratings a week. And there are many cases where such scheduling considerations have their desired effect. In other cases, however, significant numbers of viewers have changed the channel anyway.

Let us look at a week's worth of prime-time Nielsen ratings for the main American networks. Figure 1 shows the schedule for (from left to right reading vertically) ABC, CBS, NBC, and the Fox Network for December 14 to 20, 2000. You can see that NBC did very well on Thursday, but that its strong lineup did not prevent it from losing the 9:00 time slot. Through people turning their sets on or off or changing channels, the second half of *Who Wants to Be a Millionaire* drew a larger audience. Sunday belonged to CBS until 9:30, when clearly many people were more interested in the second half of another *Who Wants to Be a Millionaire* episode than in a Christmas special. In general you can see why ABC pushed *Who Wants to Be a Millionaire*—it was virtually the only ratings winner the network had, and it was very easy to tune in during the middle of it because of its game-show format. For December 18 to 20, the scheduling flow was less successful. CBS started strong on Monday evening, but football won the later hours for ABC. On Tuesday the high ratings shifted again, with ABC leading its time slot with its popular game show and one of its few successful comedies, *Dharma and Greg*. But the new *Geena*

	ABC		CBS		NBC		FOX	
THURS.		9.0/14		3.8/6		15.5/23		2.7/4
8:00	Whose Line Is It...? (R)	5.4/9	Snowden's Christmas (R)	3.9/6	Friends	15.1/24	CinderElmo (R)	2.7/4
8:30	Whose Line Is It...?	6.9/11	Garfield's Christmas (R)	4.6/7	Weber	11.5/18	(2.7/4)	2.7/4
9:00	Who Wants to Be a	12.0/18	City of Angels	4.2/6	Will & Grace	13.5/20	Olive/Reindeer (R)	2.8/4
9:30	Millionaire (12.9/19)	13.9/21	(4.4/7)	4.7/7	Just Shoot Me	12.6/19	(2.7/4)	2.6/4
10:00	Primetime Thursday	8.3/13	Sports Illustrated	2.8/4	ER	19.7/31		
10:30	(8.0/13)	7.7/13	Sportsman/Year (2.7/4)	2.6/4	(20.2/32)	20.7/34		
FRI.		5.2/9		7.6/13		9.8/17		5.5/9
8:00	Two Guys & a Girl	4.4/8	Scott Hamilton's Farewell	6.9/12	Providence	8.6/15	White House Tour	6.5/12
8:30	Two Guys & a Girl (R)	4.0/7	to Stars on Ice (7.1/13)	7.3/13	(9.0/16)	9.5/16	(6.7/12)	7.0/12
9:00	Norm	4.0/7	CSI (R)	8.4/15	Dateline	9.3/16	Greatest Christmas	4.5/8
9:30	Madigan Men	3.7/6	(8.5/15)	8.6/15	(10.1/17)	10.9/19	Moments (R) (4.2/7)	3.9/7
10:00	20/20	7.5/13	Nash Bridges	7.3/13	Law & Order: SVU	10.2/18		
10:30	(7.6/14)	7.8/14	(7.3/13)	7.3/13	(10.4/18)	10.7/19		
SAT.		5.6/10		7.2/13		4.0/7		5.7/10
8:00	The Preacher's Wife (R)	4.8/9	That's Life	5.7/11	It's A Wonderful Life	3.7/7	Cops: Jacksonville	5.1/10
8:30	(5.6/10)	5.3/10	(5.7/11)	5.7/10	(R) (4.0/7)	3.6/7	Cops: Albuquerque (R)	5.9/11
9:00			5.4/10	Walker: Texas Ranger	6.3/11		3.9/7	America's Most Wanted	5.9/11
9:30			5.7/10	(6.6/12)	6.9/12		3.8/7	(5.8/10)	5.7/10
10:00			6.0/11	The District	8.9/16		4.2/7		
10:30			6.4/11	(9.2/16)	9.5/17		4.9/9		
SUN.		8.9/13		11.2/17		8.9/13		7.2/11
7:00	Wonderful World	4.4/7	NFL Overrun	15.0/26	The Sound of Music	6.9/12	Simpsons (R)	5.2/9
7:30	of Disney: George	5.1/8	60 Minutes (7:22)	13.1/21	(R) (8.9/14)	8.1/13	King of the Hill	6.4/10
8:00	of the Jungle	6.0/9	(13.0/21)	13.3/21		8.8/13	Simpsons	8.7/13
8:30	(R) (5.6/9)	7.0/10	Touched by an Angel	10.0/15		9.7/14	Malcolm/Middle	8.3/12
9:00	Who Wants to Be a	10.9/16	(8:22) (10.7/16)	11.9/17		9.4/14	X-Files	7.5/11
9:30	Millionaire (11.7/17)	12.6/18	The Christmas Secret	9.7/14		10.1/14	(7.3/10)	7.1/10
10:00	The Practice	12.4/19	(9:22) (9.5/15)	9.3/14		9.2/14		
10:30	(12.7/20)	13.0/21		9.3/15		8.9/14		
		8.7/13		8.1/12		8.8/13		5.9/9
MON.		12.4/19		9.6/14		6.2/9		5.3/8
8:00	20/20 Downtown	8.3/14	King of Queens (R)	9.4/15	Titans*	4.2/7	Boston Public (R)	4.9/8
8:30	(8.0/13)	7.7/12	Yes, Dear	9.1/14	(4.2/6)	4.1/6	(5.0/8)	5.2/8
9:00	Monday Night Football:	13.2/20	Everybody/Raymond (R)	13.2/19	Dateline	5.7/8	Ally McBeal (R)	5.5/8
9:30	St. Louis-Tampa Bay	15.2/23	Becker	11.7/17	(6.3/9)	6.8/10	(5.5/8)	5.5/8
10:00	(9:09) (15.2/26)	16.2/25	Family Law (R)	7.3/11	Third Watch	7.8/12		
10:30		14.4/23	(7.2/12)	7.1/12	(8.1/13)	8.3/14		
TUES.		10.1/15		9.9/15		5.9/9		5.9/9
8:00	Who Wants to Be a	13.5/21	JAG (R)	7.7/12	Michael Richards*	4.0/6	That '70s Show	7.3/12
8:30	Millionaire (14.5/23)	15.6/24	(7.6/12)	7.5/12	3rd Rock	4.6/7	Titus	6.3/10
9:00	Dharma & Greg	9.9/15	60 Minutes II	9.6/15	Frasier (R)	7.3/11	Dark Angel (R)	4.9/8
9:30	Geena Davis	8.3/13	(9.8/15)	9.9/15	DAG	6.0/9	(4.9/8)	4.9/8
10:00	Once and Again	6.7/11	Judging Amy	12.0/19	Dateline	6.3/10		
10:30	(6.6/11)	6.4/11	(12.2/20)	12.5/21	(6.7/11)	7.1/12		
WED.		9.1/14		5.8/9		10.9/17		4.5/7
8:00	Who Wants to Be a	12.4/20	Bette	4.9/8	Ed	7.7/13	How to Marry a	4.5/7
8:30	Millionaire (13.4/22)	14.3/23	The Bodyguard (R)	4.7/7	(8.0/13)	8.3/13	Billionaire (4.5/7)	4.2/7
9:00	Drew Carey	9.3/14	(6.2/10)	6.2/10	West Wing	11.6/18		4.7/7
9:30	Spin City	7.6/12		6.0/9	(12.1/19)	12.6/19		4.7/7
10:00	Gideon's Crossing	5.6/9		6.3/10	Law & Order	12.5/20		
10:30	(5.5/9)	5.5/9		6.7/11	(12.6/21)	12.8/22		

Figure 1   Nielsen ratings, December 14–20, 2000. First-place ratings are indicated by shaded areas. Figures in parentheses indicate program average. (P) indicates premiere. (R) indicates rerun. All live events are listed in Eastern Time. *Source:* Nielsen Media Research.

Davis Show was not popular, despite this lead-in. Some viewers at least were willing to join *60 Minutes II* in the middle and stay tuned for the popular *Judging Amy*. A similar pattern split Saturday evening's viewership. So we see that flow as a scheduling strategy is only partly successful—primarily because all networks have the same goal of making viewers switch away from their rivals' programs.[19] Whatever the applicability of flow to various scheduling phenomena, however, there is no obvious reason why academics should model their analytical methods on a scheduling tactic.

As I have suggested, flow does not describe a typical viewer's experience even if he or she does stay tuned to one channel. Williams and many other analysts seem to presuppose that viewers mentally meld commercials and other interruptions into a seamless whole with programs, creating new meanings by the juxtapositions, deliberate or unintentional, between ads and narratives. One analysis that had a considerable impact when it appeared in 1985 dealt with a single episode of *Fantasy Island* and considered the program and commercials as a single unit in which the commercials echo the main narrative thematically and structurally: "On this episode of 'Fantasy Island,' as the narrative moves from problem to solution, from disequilibrium to equilibrium, from search to discovery, the product is there at every step, showing the way, providing therapy for what ails the characters in the commercials and, less obviously, in the program as well." The authors can find such coincidence among the various commercials and the program because they use extremely general patterns (problem/solution and so on) that are virtually universal in narratives.[20]

Yet it seems evident that most viewers can easily recognize the boundaries between the segments of a program and the commercials. Empirical research has shown that by the age of five, most children have learned to differentiate between commercials and programs; by seven or eight, they understand that advertisements are designed to persuade them to do something.[21] Certainly the vast majority of adults perceive the commercials and other added items as interruptions to their viewing of the program. I doubt they find similarities between the ads and the shows, except in the rare case of an obvious, often ironic juxtaposition, say, an ad for automated window blinds following a story of homeless people. Rather than perceiving the narrative as flowing into and incorporating the commercials, they most likely think of it as being suspended for the duration and resuming after the break ends.

There are many straightforward indications to support this view. Often commercial breaks are prefaced at the end of a segment by an announcer stating, "We'll be right back after this commercial break." Fade-outs and fade-ins usually prepare us for the end of the narrative segment that leads into the break and the beginning of the one that resumes afterward. Musical cues, a dramatic high point in the action, or a shot of a familiar locale are other conventional lead-ins to the break and to the resumption of the narrative.

I can think of no reason why we should assume people would automatically cope with such interruptions by incorporating them into what went on before. On a commonsense level, everyone knows that many viewers treat commercial breaks as intermissions that allow them to visit the toilet, raid the refrigerator, or let the

dog out. They are often welcome breaks, precisely because viewers know that the narrative is suspended briefly and that they will
miss nothing by dashing away for the few minutes such activities
consume.

More generally, let us reflect for a moment on how we cope
with interruptions in real life. Imagine that you are sitting at a
desk reading or filing clippings or learning a new computer program. The phone rings, and you stop what you are doing. You
may talk on the phone for several minutes on a topic wholly unre-
lated to what you had been doing. When you hang up and return
to your task, most likely you need only a brief glance at what you
had already done to resume it at the point you had reached. Now
imagine again that you are reading, filing, or learning a computer
program. This time a friend strolls in and says, "I'm famished.
How about stopping for some lunch?" Here you are likely to say,
"Great, but let me finish this chapter" or "let me file these last few
articles" or "let me save what I've done so far." Given a choice, we
prefer to be interrupted at a logical stopping place because it aids
our memory when we return to the job. That, I would suggest, is
how most television programs work: their breaks come at logical
stopping places, helping us to resume following the events of a
narrative.

As far as I know, psychologists have devoted little or no research to the effects of interruptions on the comprehension of
narratives. Some clinical experiments, however, have yielded results that may be relevant. First, it has been shown that if one is
learning material A and is interrupted by material B, the more un-
like the original material the interrupting material is, the easier it
will be to recall material A.[22] That is, if we are memorizing a
sonnet and are asked to look at a list of numbers, we will recall the
sonnet better than if we had been asked to look at a second son-

net. Commercials usually are quite different in type from the contents of a narrative program, with new actors, locales, subject matter, and so on. Thus they probably have relatively little impact on our ability to resume watching and understanding the narrative. Moreover, narratives seem to be one of the easiest kinds of information to remember. If people are asked to memorize strings of abstract items, such as a complex algebraic equation, they are far better able to remember them if they make up a little story about the individual items.[23] These two aspects of memory imply that we are well equipped to deal with commercial interruptions.

The implications of such abilities are obvious. Despite the prominence of the concept of flow in television studies, the individual program can be usefully studied as a self-contained unit, apart from the original schedule in which it may have appeared. This is not to say that this is the only way to study it, but certainly it is not as unproductive as some commentators assume.

I should emphasize at this point that the concept of flow has not dominated the field entirely. Many analyses of individual series and episodes have been done without regard to viewing strips, commercials, and other aspects of flow. Most of these, however, have interpreted primarily the content of these programs, usually with an orientation toward the political struggles of women, ethnic minorities, the working class, and other groups. What I am emphasizing here is something rarer: the formal analysis of television. I shall be looking at storytelling techniques that may help constitute the specificity or at least the salient differences characterizing television. Although the storytelling capacities of television may share certain traits with drama or films, there are probably differences as well. My purpose here will be to test that hypothesis by using film as my comparison point.

CLASSICAL FILM, CLASSICAL TELEVISION

In analyzing mainstream commercial television fiction, the most obviously comparable type of film is what has been called the "classical Hollywood cinema." This term refers to a stable set of norms of storytelling that were formulated during the early years of the cinema, primarily in the period from about 1909 to 1917. As David Bordwell, Janet Staiger, and I argued in our book *The Classical Hollywood Cinema*, these norms provided the means to make unified, easily comprehensible, entertaining films. So successful have Hollywood films been internationally that this system remained largely intact until at least 1960, with minor variations added along the way. In *Storytelling in the New Hollywood*, I argued further that the norms in widespread use in recent decades are essentially still those of the "Golden Age" of studio filmmaking in the decades before 1960. This is not to say that all films draw on all aspects of that model, and certainly there are some films that stretch the conventions. I mean rather that the norms are still there to be drawn on, and most films do. Here I would like to take one further step and suggest that many of these norms have been adopted or adapted by television precisely because they have been so suited to telling straightforward, entertaining stories.

Before laying out what the primary norms of storytelling are, however, I shall explain briefly the application of the word "classical" to popular film and television. This usage is not based simply on the fact that initially film and later television have employed the same basic techniques and formulas for nearly a century with so little change. It stems also from the fact that both television and film came into being in an era during which there was a huge expansion of popular storytelling media in general. During the late nineteenth century, the cheap popular-fiction magazine spread through both the U.S. and Britain. In the U.S., touring dramatic companies presented well-known plays like *Uncle Tom's Cabin* in all but the smallest towns. Along with this expansion came a need for many more writers to generate stories. In learning their trade, these writers turned to simplified versions of classical notions of what constitutes a story. In particular, Aristotle's strictures concerning beginnings, middles, and ends, and his views on unity have been widely repeated in how-to manuals for every narrative art. This Aristotelian approach has retained its force until today. The most recent screenplay manuals will invariably invoke Aristotle as a starting point for learning story structure. (I discuss such manuals' advice in Chapter 2.) Thus discussion of "classical" narrative in television is not wholly whimsical. It stems from film's and television's historical origins.

To illustrate these storytelling principles, I have chosen one successful example from film and one from television. I am not claiming that the film *Jurassic Park* (1993) is a masterpiece, though I do admire many aspects of it. I think some of the acting is overdone, and the plotline requiring Dr. Grant to learn to love children is simplistic. In general, however, the story perfectly exemplifies classical techniques. For my television example, I have chosen an episode from *The Bob Newhart Show*, one of the best American situation comedies.

In *Storytelling in the New Hollywood*, I described the core of classical storytelling in this way:

Hollywood favors unified narratives, which means most fundamentally that a cause should lead to an effect and that effect in turn should become a cause, for another effect, in an unbroken chain across the film. That is not to say that each effect follows immediately from its cause. On the contrary, one of the main sources of clarity and forward impetus in a plot is the "dangling cause," information or action which leads to no effect or resolution until later in the film.[24]

This notion of the dangling cause is particularly important, since the whole notion of certain narrative lines being temporarily suspended seems to be largely unknown in television studies. As we shall see in Chapter 2, this technique contributes a great deal to our ability to follow narratives across interruptions, including commercial breaks.

To take a simple example from *Jurassic Park*, after the Tyrannosaurus rex attack at the film's center, paleontologist Alan Grant rescues John Hammond's granddaughter, Lex; the car in which her brother Tim has been riding falls over the edge of an embankment. There follows a scene in the park's control room, where the villainous Nedry's sabotage of the park's computers (which itself picks up on a dangling cause) has baffled the technicians. On the return to Grant and Lex, we easily remember that Tim is in need of rescue from the car, now lodged in a tree. We are able to pick up even on causes that are left dangling for many scenes, especially if they are presented vividly or redundantly.

Unity and clarity require that everything in the film should be "motivated," that is, justified in some way. Motivation often involves "planting" information to be used later. Twice in *Jurassic Park* we are shown or told that Lex is a computer geek, a skill that allows her quickly to reboot the park's security systems during the film's climax—something no one else has been able to accomplish.

As this example suggests, the Hollywood cinema also bases the action closely on the traits of the characters. Causes arise almost entirely from the characters' traits and actions and only occasionally from suprapersonal forces like floods and fires. Even the dinosaurs in *Jurassic Park*, which provide so much action, are there only as a result of Hammond's entrepreneurship, and each of them, benign or aggressive, behaves as its species would dictate. As soon as the characters appear, or even before we see them, they will be assigned a set of definite traits, and our first impressions of those traits will last through the film; that is, the characters act consistently. Hammond is first seen bubbling over with enthusiasm, eager to solicit support for his project of breeding dinosaurs. He retains his optimism even in the face of setbacks and completely abandons his dreams only at the very end. If we see characters doing something that seems to run counter to their traits, some explanation will usually be given. In *Jurassic Park*, the lawyer is established in the second scene as conservative and concerned with the bottom line; he is very critical of Hammond's park and inclined to withdraw the investors' backing. Fairly quickly, however, he becomes Hammond's biggest supporter. This abrupt change is explained by his first sight of the dinosaurs, when he mutters, awestruck, "We're gonna make a fortune with this place." Even in moments of emotion, he thinks in monetary terms.

In virtually all cases, the main character in a classical Hollywood film desires something, and that desire provides the forward impetus for the narrative. We can call this figure the *goal-oriented protagonist*. Almost invariably, the protagonist's goals define the main lines of action. In *Jurassic Park*, there is no single protagonist, but Hammond's attempts to establish a dinosaur-based park determines the main plotline. Most films actually have at least two major lines of action, and the double plotline is another distinctive feature of the Hollywood cinema. As we all know, romance is central to nearly all Hollywood films, and typically one line of action involves a romance, while the other concerns some other goal of the protagonist. These two goals are usually causally linked. In *Jurassic Park*, the second line of action stems from Ellie's goal of reconciling Grant, her fiancé, to the idea of having children, and as he gradually develops a loving and protective attitude toward Hammond's grandchildren, her goal is achieved. Although the couple are already engaged at the beginning of the film, the prospects for a happy marriage have increased by the end. Ellie's goal relates to the main plot in a simple fashion, through the danger into which the park plunges all the characters. Villains, of course, also have goals, and the clash between these and the positive characters' goals creates much of the narrative's conflict. Nedry's desire for wealth causes him to steal the dinosaur embryos and shut down the park's security and communications systems.

Again, the idea of goals seems obvious, yet there are types of films that do not use this strategy. In the European art cinema, for example, characters often act because they are forced to, not because they want to. Michelangelo Antonioni has made a number of films where the protagonists seem unable to actively pursue their goals. *L'Avventura* (1960), for example, involves a search and a tentative romance, both of which would be the kinds of goals common in Hollywood films; yet the film concentrates on the psychological inability of the characters to follow through on these goals. In other art films, characters may conceive goals but never achieve them, as in Jaco Van Dormaël's *Toto le héros* (1991). In Chapter 4, I discuss films and television programs that use a similar approach to goals.

In addition to their overall definite, linear causality, part of the appeal of Hollywood films stems from their ease of comprehension on a scene-to-scene level. Keeping the ongoing causality, time, and space intelligible across transitions is particularly important in the media involving moving images. A cut can transport us instantly from one scene to a new space containing an action involving different characters, taking place at a different time. Several techniques keep us from being disoriented by these changes.

A simple but effective device is the *dialogue hook*, a line spoken at the end of one scene that prepares us for what happens next. At the end of the scene where the avuncular Hammond shows his guests the dinosaurs for the first time, Grant asks, "How'd you do this?" Hammond responds, "I'll show you." The next scene shows the characters arriving at the visitors' center and watching a presentation on dinosaur DNA. Here the same characters are involved, and the action continues in a nearby space after a brief ellipsis. Early in the film, however, a more potentially disorienting transition occurs. The lawyer visits an amber mine and mentions Grant's name to a minor character, the mine foreman. The latter remarks, "Grant's like me. He's a digger." There is a sudden shift to shots of brushes clearing sand from a fossil skeleton. This is a new locale, and Grant has not yet appeared in the film, but we are prepared to understand that the man we next see is Grant, a digger, and that this site is where he digs. A title identifies it for us: "Badlands. Near Snakewater, Montana." Such expository writing, by the way, whether through superimposed titles like this one or signs within the setting, have helped establish a new locale since the silent-film era.

Temporal relations are often made comprehensible by the use of a *deadline*—a device that often serves to build suspense as well. *Jurassic Park* has two long-range deadlines. Hammond is initially given forty-eight hours to prove the viability of his park to the visiting experts. In this case the deadline is not met, since circumstances force him to abandon his goal. The villainous computer expert Nedry also has a deadline: he must get the stolen dinosaur embryos to a ship that is leaving at seven o'clock. Moreover, the transport device will keep the embryos alive for only thirty-six hours. Nedry misses this deadline, but rushing to meet the ship is what causes him to go astray and be killed by a dinosaur. Characters in films also often make appointments, which usually provide a short-term sense of how much time has passed between scenes.

One means for fixing important causes or lines of action vividly in our minds is the *motif*. Films tend to use visual motifs that become emblematic of an important idea. For example, when we see Grant terrify a child early on, he uses a fossil velociraptor claw to illustrate his grisly account of the dinosaur's killing methods (Figure 2). We see him handling it a couple of scenes later, as he and Ellie sit in the helicopter across from Malcolm (Figure 3); Grant will soon become jealous when this new acquaintance begins flirting with Ellie. Thus the claw becomes associated with

Figure 2

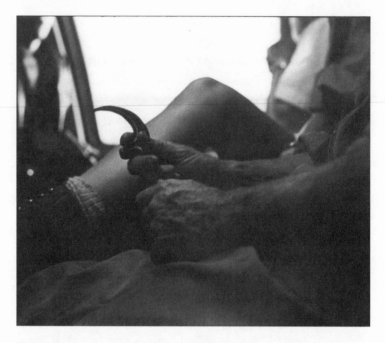

Figure 3

Grant's obsession with his work and unfriendly attitude toward most other people. (His first reaction to Hammond's appearance at the excavation site had been anger.) Finally, as he plays a fatherly role by guarding the two sleeping children, he tosses the claw away (Figure 4). Thus the point is underscored with a motif that is not causally important in itself but that traces a character change. Similarly, a verbal motif is Hammond's chipper line as he displays aspects of the park, "Spared no expense!" He says this four times before finally repeating it softly and with a touch of sad irony as he and Ellie sit eating melting ice cream and she explains why his dream is impossible.

While not all classical films employ motifs as carefully as *Jurassic Park* does, virtually all aid viewer comprehension by conveying

Figure 4

important information redundantly. An event may be mentioned by a character as about to occur, we may then see it occur, and other characters may then discuss it. We do not actually see the velociraptors until late in *Jurassic Park*, but the death of a worker in the opening sequence and the episode of a live cow being lowered into the raptor cage and torn apart amply demonstrate how dangerous they are. Moreover, the Kenyan gamekeeper explains the raptors' mode of hunting in detail, expressing a reluctant admiration for their intelligence and skill. By the time the raptors start attacking the main characters, we are well primed to understand this new threat.

Similarly, character traits are often established and reiterated several times. Immediately after Grant is introduced, he deliberately frightens a rude child among a group of tourists by describing a velociraptor attack, as previously mentioned. Soon after, his fiancée, Ellie, who wants to have children, chides him for this, and he lists some of his objections to children. In case we missed all this, it is mentioned briefly in the next scene, where Hammond is describing his park to the pair: "Our attractions will drive kids out of their minds." Grant responds, "And what are those?" Ellie, willfully misunderstanding, teases him by answering, "Small versions of adults, honey." When the group climbs into the vehicles for the tour of the park, Grant evades the hero-worshipping Tim, who has latched onto him, by tricking him into sitting in the other car. Thus by the time Grant ends up alone with the kids in the jungle, we are well aware of the fact that he does not like children. We also strongly suspect that he will learn to love them, since that is Ellie's goal.

The techniques of classical cinema I have been describing can be found in television as well. In order briefly to demonstrate this claim, I shall look at an episode of *The Bob Newhart Show* called "Big Brother Is Watching" (1974). The action primarily involves Ellen, sister of the psychologist Bob Hartley, and her attempts to find an apartment in Chicago. When she fails and decides to move in with her boyfriend Howard, Bob's objections create bad feelings among the characters. Here is a scene-by-scene summary of the action:

"Big Brother Is Watching"

CREDITS

[COMMERCIAL BREAK]

SCENE 1 (Bob and Emily's apartment) Bob's sister Ellen has recently moved to Chicago and is living with their mother. She can't stand this and wants her own apartment. Her boyfriend Howard offers to let her stay with him, but she feels she has known him too briefly. She accepts Emily's offer to let her stay temporarily with her and Bob and makes an *appointment* to go apartment hunting with Emily the next day.

SCENE 2   Bob and Emily prepare to sleep in their den while Ellen has their bedroom; Bob complains about this arrangement.

SCENE 3   (Bob's office) Carol, the receptionist, tells the dentist, Jerry, that she has been taking gourmet cooking classes and makes an *appointment* to have him over for dinner on Tuesday. Ellen visits Bob and tells him that Emily has been bossy during their apartment hunting and she has decided to move in with Howard after all. Bob claims to accept this.

SCENE 4   (Bob and Emily's apartment) Ellen prepares to move her things across the hall to Howard's place. Bob suddenly threatens Howard if they continue.

[COMMERCIAL BREAK]

SCENE 4 cont.   Howard refuses to take Ellen's side, not wanting to alienate his best friend. Upset, Ellen stalks out.

SCENE 5   (Bob's office) Carol mentions to Bob that Ellen is now staying at her apartment; Ellen appears and says she is still angry with Bob and Howard.

SCENE 6   Jerry comes into Bob's office and is offended when Bob calls Howard his "best friend." Bob realizes all his friends are upset with him.

SCENE 7   At home in her apartment, Carol, in curlers and robe, orders a pizza to be delivered (having forgotten her invitation to Jerry). Emily and then Bob come in, hoping to see Ellen, who is not home. Jerry arrives for the promised gourmet dinner (set up in Scene 3). Carol retires to get dressed. Howard arrives to apologize to Ellen. Ellen enters and says she has found an apartment of her own. All exit to see her place and have dinner together. Carol appears, dressed up, and Emily returns to invite her to join the group.

[COMMERCIAL BREAK]

TAG   (Bob and Emily's apartment) Ellen and Howard are having coffee with Bob and Emily late one night. Howard offers to let her stay with him, and Bob objects. Howard and Ellen leave.

As in the typical classical Hollywood film, the causal action here all arises from the characters' goals and traits. We know Bob to be fussy, a bit repressed, and embarrassed by open displays of emotion; he also dislikes interfering in people's lives—except those of his patients. Thus it is perfectly in character for him to pretend to accept Ellen's decision to live with Howard and then suddenly reveal that he actually opposes it. Bob's wife Emily is an extremely pleasant person, but from past episodes we know that she is something of a busybody, enjoying advising others and matchmaking for friends. At the end of scene 1, as she serves dinner, Emily starts listing all the things she and Ellen will do tomorrow, including apartment hunting. Her line "It's Ellen's life, and she has to decide how she wants to live it" comically points up her bossiness and plants the motivation for Ellen's failure to find an apartment the next day and her decision to stop hunting and move in with Howard even though she had said she felt it was too soon. Emily's excessive, interfering kindness also motivates the otherwise implausible situation of her giving Ellen the master bedroom while she and Bob sleep on the pull-out couch in the den. Howard is impetuous and illogical, and his attempts to persuade Ellen to live with him when they know each other so little stem from what we know of him. (Their whirlwind courtship figured in an earlier episode.) Ellen, though a relatively new character in the series at this point, has been established as more steady and sensible than Howard.

Even viewers who have never seen an episode of this series could grasp all these traits fairly easily, as they are all demonstrated or hinted at in the course of the program. In Chapter 2 I discuss how television exposition and redundancy must function to provide new viewers with already-established narrative information of this sort.

Despite the fact that the program's action runs only twenty-four minutes, like a film, it has two plotlines. Indeed, in television production there are terms for these: the main storyline is the A plot, and the subsidiary line is the B plot (with C, D, and so on, for any additional plotlines).[25]

In "Big Brother Is Watching," the A plot involves Ellen's search for a place to live in Chicago. This search is the narrative's main goal, and it is motivated thoroughly. Initially Ellen is living with her mother, but within the first minute of the action Bob says: "Well, I know my mother, and I know my sister, and I don't see them lasting more than a week." Thus personality clashes are set up as the main driving force in this plot. Ellen enters immediately and says, "I cannot live with that woman!" This plotline will be resolved in the final scene when Ellen finds her own apartment.

Plot B is set up at the beginning of scene 3, over a quarter of the way through. It seems initially merely a bit of comic relief: Carol boasts about how she is learning gourmet cooking and invites Jerry to dinner on Tuesday night. This appointment is barely mentioned until the end, but it provides a dangling cause that keeps the B plot going. The dinner also provides a time frame for the plot, since the climax takes place at Carol's apartment on Tuesday night. Finally, this scene also suggests that she does not have much of a social life, since her datebook is nearly blank. Like the other characters, Carol behaves consistently with her traits. From past episodes we know that she is single and constantly on the lookout for men; she sometimes occupies her evenings with pursuits like the cooking class. As is characteristic of a classical film, the two narrative lines are causally connected, and in this case plot A and plot B also create a structural contrast: Carol has an apartment but no boyfriend; Ellen has a boyfriend but no apartment.

The B plot resurfaces briefly in scene 5, where Carol's dialogue informs us that Ellen is temporarily living with her while pursuing her goal of finding her own place. Even though the dinner with Jerry is not mentioned, the idea of Carol inviting Ellen to stay with her may recall that appointment; at any rate, it broadens the B plot to focus on Carol's having guests at her apartment. The point of having the B plot in this episode at all becomes clear in the climactic scene 7; there it dovetails tidily with the A plot. The dangling causes from both plotlines draw all the characters together for a series of explanations and apologies and a final resolution of the A plot when Ellen announces she has found her own apartment and the happy group exits to see it. The B plot still has to work itself out, however, for Carol bustles out, now dressed and made up, only to find herself once more apparently abandoned to a lonely evening. The last minute of scene 7 resolves the B plot in this way:

Ellen, Bob, Howard, Emily, and Jerry go out the door of Carol's apartment.

JERRY: "Maybe we can get our 'best friend' [i.e., Bob] to pick up the tab, huh?"

Emily laughs; Jerry closes the door behind the group. With a "Ta da!" Carol emerges from the bedroom and strikes a pose to show off her carefully done hair and gauzy, green floor-length dress. She looks around in surprise, then immediately begins gesturing and speaking to an imaginary guest about her outfit.

CAROL: "Oh, you really like it? Thank you so much. It's a little something I picked up today at Carson's."

She moves about as if among a group of guests.

CAROL: "Oh, thank you, thank you! I know, green has always been very kind to me. The shoes? Why, no, they're not new, but you know, they never seem to go out of style."

She sits on the sofa. A knock.

CAROL, *crossing to the door:* "Oh, just a minute! Who is it?"

EMILY, *off:* "It's Emily."

CAROL: "Oh, Emily!"

She opens the door, and Emily enters.

EMILY: "Oh, honey, we are so sorry! We were all just getting in the car, and we realized that we'd left you up here alone. Come on now. We're all going out to dinner."

CAROL: "Oh, thanks. I'd love to."

She crosses to get her coat. Emily follows, looking at her outfit.

EMILY: "Oh, Carol, I *love* that dress."

CAROL: "Oh, thank you. It's just a little something I picked up at Carson's."

EMILY: "Oh, it's a wonderful color."

CAROL: "Really, you think so? Green has always been very kind to me."

EMILY: "And those shoes! Are they new?"

CAROL: "No, they're not new, but you know, they never go out of style."

They go out and close the door.

This resolution does double duty. First, it provides a social life for Carol (while displaying the resilient humor that is one of her established traits) and lets us stop feeling sorry for her. Second, it allows us to go away with a more positive view of Emily. Emily is ordinarily quite likable, but in this episode she has shown her main flaw by bossing Ellen around and criticizing her taste in apartments. Now Emily returns and pays Carol a series of compliments that not only cheer Carol up but re-emphasize that Emily is basically a good person.

The scene-to-scene progression through this episode is quite clear. There are no dialogue hooks, but most scenes begin with a shot of the exterior of the building in which the action will occur. Since the same establishing shots are used in most episodes, they are quite familiar and cue us as to where we are. Indeed, the opening shot of the standard credit sequence, Bob leaving his office and folding up a sign reading "Group in session," instantly identifies him for any new viewers as a psychologist. (Like most sitcoms, *The Bob Newhart Show* uses a limited number of settings over and over.) The dangling causes and Carol's dinner appointment help give a sense of the plot's taking place over a period of a few days.

Although "Big Brother Is Watching" has no visual motifs comparable to the dinosaur-claw imagery in *Jurassic Park*, it creates other parallels through repetition. The "best friend" motif begins as Jerry becomes offended at Bob's reference to Howard as his best friend, and it returns in the scene just quoted. Similarly, dining with friends and family frames the film, with Bob and Emily hosting Ellen and Howard at the beginning, Carol offering Jerry a gourmet meal, and the whole group celebrating their various happy endings by going out to a restaurant at the end.

This short analysis demonstrates that film and television share some of the same techniques for creating clear and unified narratives. I suspect that applying the concept of flow to "Big Brother Is Watching" would obscure the deftness of its plotting. You may notice that although I included the commercial breaks in the scene breakdown, I did not mention how they fit into the narrative structure. Obviously, I do not believe that the commercials that occupied those breaks "flowed" into the storyline itself. I do not think, however, that these breaks have no effect at all on the narrative. On the contrary, in creating television episodes for commercial television, screenwriters definitely take these breaks into account in planning structure. Such breaks and their impact on narrative take us into a new area, however: the differences in storytelling strategies between television and film. I turn to those differences in Chapter 2.

2

WHAT DO THEY THINK THEY'RE DOING? THEORY AND PRACTICE IN SCREENWRITING

PRINCIPLES AND STRATEGIES OF TELEPLAY WRITING

Chapter 1 may have left you with the impression that a narrow focus on the concept of "flow" has largely precluded theoretical work on the structure of television narrative. Fortunately, there does exist a body of such work, though it has not been generated within what one would call television studies proper. I refer to the manuals devoted to teaching aspiring authors how to go about writing "teleplays," as scripts for television are called. These manuals are in some cases the product of successful teleplay writers and in others of teachers in university scriptwriting courses. Although such manuals are certainly not high-level theory, on a practical level they can tell us much about the aesthetic norms of commercial television. They often lay out primary conventions very explicitly. We find some advice given over and over in several manuals, providing good evidence that the techniques discussed are normative within the industry. The best of them can give us helpful indications of what to look for in specific programs.

Much of what they tell us closely resembles the techniques described in Chapter 1 as typical of classical Hollywood films. Television plots depend on strong chains of action—causes and effects generated by characters and motivated by those characters' traits and goals. Indeed, some scenario manuals deal with both film and television. There are, however, major differences in narrative structure between television and film, and the manuals might be a good place to start seeking them.

The main drawback of these manuals is that they are aimed at aspiring freelancers rather than established writers, and hence they stick to a fairly rudimentary level. They do not deliver us a ready-made guide to all the features of television narrative. For example, television programs spend a fair amount of time recapping previous action, not just at the beginning of programs but within them as well, for the people who might happen to tune in at any moment. Few manuals discuss this special demand of teleplay scripting, primarily, I suspect, because their aim is simply to coach the beginner in writing a presentable portfolio script. I shall deal with the issue of redundant and dispersed exposition later in this chapter.

In chapter 1, I briefly defended the application of the term "classical" to narratives in popular film and television. Like the writing manuals devoted to film, those for teleplay writers almost invariably cite Aristotle to justify their advice on issues of unity, motivation, and the fact that stories must have beginnings, middles, and ends. Here, for example, the author of a book on writing situation comedies discusses the standard plot pattern:

This pattern of development is nothing new. It's the same linear structure model that was described by Aristotle over two thousand years ago. To paraphrase from *Aristotle's Politics & Poetics* (a book that you should probably have on your shelf), a story is composed of three sections: a *beginning* introduces a complication to a character's life, launching the story. The *middle* section presents developing action, a series of *revolutions* and *discoveries*, which drives the story forward. The *end* resolves the story conflict, often through a reversal of fortune for the main character.[1]

Describing a very different form, the daytime soap opera, another teleplay adviser deals with motivation and coincidence:

> Speaking to us across the millennia, Aristotle tells us in *Poetics*, regarding events that arouse pity or fear, "Such incidents have the very greatest effect on the mind *when they occur unexpectedly and at the same time in consequence of one another; there is more of the marvelous in them then than if they happened by themselves or by mere chance. Even matters of chance seem most marvelous if there is an appearance of design, as it were, in them* [italics mine]."

The author plausibly concludes, "I can't think of anyone since who has put it as well."[2] Manuals, then, are quite consciously Aristotelian in much of the advice they offer—in part no doubt to lend themselves an aura of authority.

Aristotelian principles, however, have to be adjusted to the constraints of the medium to which they are applied. Many teleplay manuals offer detailed, often daunting descriptions of the practical conditions of writing for television. Some brief examples of typical constraints will suggest why so much television tends to adhere to formulaic narrative structure. Such examples may also, however, give us more respect for those writers who manage to work creatively within such limitations.

Most obviously, authors must stick to much more exact time frames than if they were writing theatrical films. Films can present anywhere from 85 to 140 minutes of advertisement-free action, with three hours not uncommon in recent years. In contrast, the traditional "half-hour" commercial television program contains 24 minutes of actual plot action (or, recently, closer to 22), while the "hour" program contains roughly 47. Ad breaks, as we shall see, usually come at invariable times, necessitating the insertion of what are called "cliffhangers" before each one. Many sitcoms are shot on three side-by-side standing sets in front of a live audience, making scenes in other locales—especially outdoors—difficult. Hour for hour, budgets are typically much lower than those for feature films, discouraging the use of any subjects requiring elaborate special effects, large crowds, or shooting in distant locales. Most types of television programs must deal with stricter censorship standards than are typically applied to films.

Despite such restrictions on content, huge amounts of programming time must be filled each year—22 or 26 times half an hour for a successful sitcom and the same times an hour for a drama. Writers in these forms at least have a respite during part of the year when the program is in reruns. American daytime soap operas, which appear daily and do not have reruns, can last either a half or a full hour. Either type requires a staggering 260 episodes per year. Compare this with the fact that these days a film director or sceenwriter does very well to complete a single two-hour release each year.

Such huge amounts of plot can usually be generated only by

teams of writers, usually with assistants, editors, researchers, and other personnel participating in the creation of a series of scripts. A few individuals manage to write an entire series single-handed and thereby gain their peers' awed admiration. In soap opera the team-writing process becomes labyrinthine, as five separate people write the episodes for a single week, striving to make the four or five storylines of each episode link up in conformance to a long-range scene outline. At the same time these writers must keep track of the various contractual requirements of the actors. Stars have a maximum number of programs in which they will appear; lesser-known players demand a minimum number of appearances. The actors' vacations are staggered through the year, meaning that the plot must juggle their periods of unavailability.

In such circumstances, widely agreed-upon norms and guidelines are usually a necessity. Many of the distinctive narrative strategies in television arise from these unique constraints.

LARGE-SCALE PARTS

In any medium, one major creative factor is the length or scale of the individual art work. A novel is not a stretched-out short story, and a sonnet is not a long limerick. After the early years of television, when a few fifteen-minute programs were on the air, the format generally settled into a small set of conventional lengths based on half-hour, one-hour, and two-hour time slots. Each type demands a different approach to storytelling, and manuals typically handle each separately. I refer to half-hour and one-hour programs collectively as "short-form" television.

Although one-hour series programs often use two-hour episodes to premiere or end a season, the regular two-hour series is quite rare. Oxford's own *Inspector Morse* provides one instance. In fact, if we eliminate the time devoted to commercials, *Inspector Morse* episodes run closer to 104 minutes, but that still makes them comparable to feature films. This program, with its relatively high budgets, scripts by famous authors, and small number of episodes per series, has been described thus: "As long and at least as complex as most feature films, *Morse* is at times quite cinematic in its pleasures." This critic remarks on "the rather untelevisually relaxed pace of its narrative development" and points out that its popularity meant that airings of fresh episodes "assumed the status of minor public events"[3]—somewhat like that of a new movie. In November of 2000, the broadcast of the last episode was widely referred to in the press and daily conversation.

Analysis of one episode of *Inspector Morse*, "The Infernal Serpent" (episode 1 of series 4), confirms the claim that the individual installments are fairly similar to feature films. They could be analyzed using the same approach that one would use in looking at classical Hollywood films—the one exception being that the commercial breaks would necessitate a more diffused, redundant exposition, a subject I deal with later. In this book, I confine my remarks to short-form programs, as we can find more evidence for television's distinctive traits there.

Broadly speaking, half-hour series are usually sitcoms, while dramatic shows of various sorts dominate the hour-long format. This may seem a somewhat arbitrary division, and most teleplay manuals do not explain it. In an interview, Bob Weiskopf, a veteran writer of such programs as *I Love Lucy* and *All in the Family*, offers a simple reason:

It's very difficult to write an hour's worth of situation-comedy material on a weekly basis. We did it on the *Lucy/Desi Comedy Hour*, but we only did four or five a year, and we had great stars interacting with our characters. Each show took us six weeks to write. You don't have that kind of time on a weekly situation comedy.[4]

Interestingly, John Cleese and Connie Booth spent the same amount of time, roughly six weeks, writing each half-hour episode of *Fawlty Towers*—a luxury few staff writers of sitcoms have. Thus the work involved in plotting the action and devising gags seems to be the main reason why sitcoms are almost always short.

The formats of half-hour and one-hour programs in commercial televion are similar in one way. At approximately fifteen-minute intervals, there is typically a break for advertisements. Much of the advice in how-to manuals focuses on how to structure television narratives around these breaks, which divide the program into so-called acts. Madeline Dimaggio, author of scripts for *Kojak*, *The Bob Newhart Show*, and *Three's Company*, has written one of the best advice manuals I have read. She succinctly describes these act structures and how they function:

Absolutely everything in television builds to the act end. *The more powerful the act ends, the bigger the hook.*

All one-hour scripts are broken into four acts. Each act averages fourteen to fifteen pages. Each act in the hour episode is a separate unit with a crisis and climax all its own. Why? The commercial breaks are placed between acts.

The most important act, and what the producers tag the "cliffhanger," happens at the end of Act II because the break runs twice the length of the other commercials . . .

Powerful act ends are just as important in the half-hour comedy. This script is broken into two acts. The most important break is the Act I end. Here, a major complication in the plot takes place, which should leave the audience hanging . . .

Remember your goal. It's to pull 'em back from the refrigerator.[5]

Most manuals give variants of this description, though most call the end of every act except the last a "cliffhanger"; in a serial program, cliffhangers will be used at the end as well.

This use of the term "act" for a large-scale part of a television episode is similar to the way practitioners and critics describe parts of movies. In the past twenty years, it has become common to refer to feature films as having a "three-act structure." Scenario manuals universally quote the same Aristotelian formula of beginning-middle-end. The most common version of this formula was popularized by Syd Field's 1979 how-to book, *Screenplay*, often referred to in screenwriting circles as "the bible." He claimed that a two-hour film invariably contains a half-hour act at the beginning to set up the story, an hour-long middle act during which the protagonist meets obstacles, and a half-hour climactic portion at the end. The dividing points among these three acts are generally called "turning points," and Field defines a turning point as "an incident, or event, that hooks into the story and spins it around into another direction."[6]

In *Storytelling in the New Hollywood*, I take issue with this model, arguing instead that most films contain four acts of approximately thirty minutes each and that therefore there is a midway turning point as well.[7] I will not re-argue that point here, but it is interesting to note that in short-form television, acts are roughly half the length of those in feature films (assuming my four-act model) and their main turning point, or at least a cliffhanger, typically comes near the midpoint. Such mandatory large-scale divisions help shape the scene-to-scene development of episodes.

Most of us have watched enough television to have a sense of how cliffhangers work, but let me give you an example and suggest how the central break relates to the overall shape of a program. Returning to the episode of *The Bob Newhart Show* examined in Chapter 1, I would like to look at the scenes just before and after the central break. (See plot synopsis in Chapter 1.) In the first half of the episode, Ellen has fruitlessly sought an apartment and, not finding one, has decided to move in with her fiancé—apparently with her brother Bob's approval. Here is how Act I ends and Act II begins, with the fades indicating where the commercials were:

Bob reading a newspaper, Emily sewing, sitting side by side on the sofa. Ellen and Howard are about to leave.

HOWARD, *reaching down to shake Bob's hand:*   "Good-bye, Bob."

BOB: "So long, Howard."

He goes back to reading. Howard picks up Ellen's suitcase, and they move to the door.

BOB: "Howard!"

HOWARD: "Yeah?"

BOB: "Take another step, I break both your legs."

Musical sting with fade-out. Commercial break.

Fade-in to same situation with Howard, Ellen, and Emily staring at Bob, who has not raised his eyes from his paper.

HOWARD *laughs:*   "That's funny, Bob. [To Ellen] Let's go."

ELLEN: "Wait a minute, Howard. I—I don't think he's kidding."

HOWARD, *putting down the suitcase:*   "Aw, sure he's kidding. Aren't you kidding, Bob? Course he's kidding."

EMILY, *upset, to Bob:*   "Now, wait a minute. I mean, a minute ago this was OK."

BOB, *getting up and moving away from them:*   "Well, a minute ago I didn't feel this way. It just suddenly hit me. My—my kid sister in that apartment. I, well, then, then I felt this way."

This act break conforms to a common sitcom pattern described by teleplay manuals. The action builds to a point where the initial problem seems to be solved, and then a turning-point event shows that the resolution has not really been achieved; moreover, this event ratchets up the level of conflict. Now not only does Ellen have no place to live, but the group's altercation creates serious rifts among the characters. The second act increases the general antagonism and then reconciles everyone.

The *Bob Newhart* example is quite tidy, but not all turning points come just before commercials. Some sitcom episodes juggle separate cliffhangers and turning points. The American sitcom *Murphy Brown* is noted for its odd placements of commercial breaks. In 1992, the show included a series of episodes devoted to Murphy's pregnancy. In one of these, she seeks a partner to accompany her to Lamaze classes and be present at the birth. Two commercial breaks divide the episode into three acts. The first act ends about seven and a half minutes into the program. By this point we are not quite a third of the way through the plot, and Murphy has failed to persuade any of her colleagues to be her partner. Their refusals, one after another, create humor by playing off the different traits of the characters and explain why she does not continue to pursue trying to persuade one of them to be her partner. The lead-in to the first break is not exactly a cliffhanger in the sense of creating tension, but it emphasizes the dangling cause that Murphy still needs a partner:

The newsroom supervisor, Miles, has lost his initial enthusiasm for being Murphy's partner and declines, exiting; Murphy is left with her friend and colleague Frank, who has a scheduling conflict that prevents him from helping Murphy, and Corky, an enthusiastic female colleague.

FRANK: "Okay! This is not a problem. We—we've still got lots of options."

CORKY: "Of course you do! And one of them is standing right here. *I'll* be your Lamaze partner!"

MURPHY, *appalled:*   "What!?"

CORKY: "Think about it, Murphy. Who better than a woman to give you the compassion you'll need in your time of trial? And don't forget, Murphy, I was brought up on a farm. I've had my arm in a cow all the way up to here." *Tapping her arm just below the shoulder.*

FRANK, *revolted, turns and rushes away:*   "Oh!"

Murphy stands aghast as Corky continues to smile at her.

The scene's end leads to the first commercial break.

Even with its somewhat unconventional division into large-scale parts, however, this episode places its main turning point about midway through, just past the twelve-minute mark, when Eldin, the man who is perpetually painting Murphy's townhouse, agrees to be her partner:

Murphy's apartment. Eldin has been expressing doubts about becoming her Lamaze partner.

MURPHY: "I understand. As a matter of fact, I don't even know if I'm gonna take this class myself. I'm only doing it because my doctor wanted me to. Probably be a complete waste of time."

ELDIN: "Wait—wait a minute! What are you saying, that you're gonna go into this thing totally alone and unprepared? You know what a screamer you are. You'll probably alienate everyone at the hospital, create an environment of hostility, bitterness. I can't let a child be born into a room with that kind of energy."

MURPHY, *smiling:* "Eldin, are you telling me you'll do it?"

ELDIN: "I'll take the class and see how it feels, but that's all I can promise right now."

MURPHY: "Thank you. I know what a big step this is for you."

ELDIN: "What, are you kidding? The last time I made this kinda commitment, I had to buy four albums a year at regular club prices."

Dissolve to the exterior of a large building, then inside to the Lamaze classroom.

There is no commercial break here, but this moment definitely shifts the action. As we shall see, the second half deals with the Lamaze classes and their effect on Murphy's overly casual attitude toward the impending birth. That attitude has already been set up

Table 2.1   Time length of parts of *Yes, Minister* episodes

	Episode 2 "The Official Visit"	Episode 4 "Big Brother"
Credits	00:41	00:41
Act 1	13:11	13:12
First part	(7:09)	(6:20)
Second part	(6:02)	(7:01)
Act 2	13:40	14:37
First part	(7:52)	(9:41)
Second part	(5:48)	(4:56)
End credits	00:41	00:41
Total	28.13	29.11

redundantly, in the opening scene with her doctor and in this scene with Eldin.

Sitcoms on noncommercial television, such as those shown on the BBC, have more leeway for structuring their large-scale parts. Still, some have what I would consider a turning point roughly halfway through. Consider the timings of Episodes 2 and 4 of *Yes, Minister,* shown in Table 2.1. Each episode's turning point creates amazingly similar and balanced large-scale sections. The midway transition of episode 4, "Big Brother," provides an excellent example.

The episode's first half has established that the Minister of Administrative Affairs, Jim Hacker, wants to institute privacy safeguards for a new National Integrated Database, while the Machiavellian permanent undersecretary, Sir Humphrey Appleby, opposes them. The turning point comes as the secretary, Bernard, reveals that Jim can appear on a television interview show and reveal his plan to the nation. The second half begins with a scene in which Hacker meets with his predecessor and gets some advice on how to handle Sir Humphrey—information that leads to a climax involving one of Hacker's few outright triumphs over Humphrey.

Office of Jim Hacker, sitting at his desk facing Humphrey.

JIM, *uncertainly:* "I see. We don't want to do anything that wouldn't be . . ." *Flaps hand.*

HUMPHREY, *grinning, shakes his head patronizingly:* "No."

JIM: "No."

BERNARD, *Jim's secretary, off:* "Oh, excuse me, Minister."

JIM: "Yes, Bernard?"

BERNARD, *entering and crossing to stand beside the desk:* "A slight problem, Minister."

JIM: "Oh?"

BERNARD: "Yes, because of the adverse, well, that is to say, not entirely favourable press reaction to your interview last night, the other channel want you for their programme, 'World in Focus.'"

JIM: "Say no."

BERNARD: "No?"

JIM: "Yes, no."

BERNARD: "Yes, no?"

JIM: "Yes, say no. That's final!"

BERNARD: "Well, if that's what you want, Minister, but they did say, even if you didn't appear, they would go ahead with the item anyway, and there would be nobody there to state your case."

JIM: "No, okay, yes."

BERNARD: "No, okay, yes? Oh, I see what you mean."

JIM: *"Yes!"*

BERNARD: "Finally final?"

JIM, *annoyed:*   "Thank you, Bernard."

Bernard exits.

JIM: "Now! What am I going to tell *them* about safeguards, Humphrey?"

HUMPHREY, *cheekily referring to a line from Jim's earlier disastrous television appearance:*   "Well, perhaps you could remind them, Minister, that Rome wasn't built in a day."

Dissolve to a luxurious men's club. Jim carries a drink and paper across the room and recognizes the previous holder of his ministerial position dozing in a chair.

JIM: "Tom!"

TOM: "Oh! My dear fellow."

JIM: "Mind if I join you?"

TOM: "No, course not."

JIM: "Well, how are you enjoying being in opposition?"

TOM: "How are you enjoying being in government?"

JIM, *with a grimace:*   "Oh, not as much as I expected, actually. Well, not at the moment."

TOM: "Humphrey got you under control?"

JIM: "It's so hard to get things done. Did you manage to get things done?"

TOM: "Oh, almost nothing, old boy. Mind you, I didn't cotton onto his technique until after I'd been there a year, and then there was the election."

JIM: "Technique?"

TOM: "Stalling technique."

Thus it would appear that in some cases even half-hour programs that are not interrupted by commercials tend to include major turning points that divide them into large-scale parts, or acts—though obviously here the authors were not required to time these moments as precisely as they did.

With the increasing number of original series produced by "premium" channels like HBO in the U.S., one might wonder whether these commercial-free programs also fall into evenly timed acts. A look at one half-hour sitcom, *Sex and the City*, and one roughly hour-long drama, *The Sopranos*, suggests that act structure is somewhat more flexible in such programs, but that it is not abandoned or radically altered.

Based on analysis of the first eight episodes of the first season, *Sex and the City* has a fairly formulaic structure that does tend to break into two acts. The first act involves the main character, Carrie, setting out to write a column in her newspaper series "Sex and the City." Each column establishes the "issue" for the week, such as "Is there a secret cold war between marrieds and singles?" (Episode 3) or "Are men in their twenties the new designer drug?" (Episode 4). Each of her four friends (usually gathering for a meal, card game, or similar social occasion) delivers a firm opinion on the subject consistent with her established personality: Miranda states a cynical position, Samantha a hedonistic one, and Charlotte a romantic one. Carrie usually expresses her view,

Table 2.2   Time length of acts in *Sex and the City* episodes

Episode	Act 1	Act 2
1	15:01	9:51
2	13:27	9:30
3	11:34	10:15
4	11:07	10:15
5	12:09	10:39
6	9:55	11:43
7	11:16	11:25
8	9:25	12:55

though with less certainty. The B and C plots typically involve two of the three friends in some action relating to the main issue—these characters lead remarkably parallel lives—and the A plot confronts Carrie with a situation that causes her to question her original opinion.

The first acts of the first two episodes are distinctly longer than the second acts, due to the need to establish the continuing characters. By the third episode, however, the two acts are more balanced, not counting the credits (see Table 2.2). Thus the acts tend not to vary more than two minutes in either direction from the average. The act break is often signaled by a visual transition, such as a fade, elaborate wipe, or dissolve. Most plotlines achieve closure within episodes, though Carrie's ongoing romance with Mr. Big provides a continuing arc.

This flurry of activity is held together by many classical devices: appointments (dates and parties loom large), dangling causes, and dialogue hooks. Most important, Carrie's voice-over narration almost invariably establishes the time frame of each new scene ("Meanwhile," "two hours later," "the next night," and so on), as well as the locale when it is not evident from the visuals. Carrie also makes asides to the audience to clarify the action. Thus subsidiary plots, which often involve only a few brief scenes, weave swiftly together to create an impression of dense action.

The Sopranos is more complex and flexible. For one thing, the episodes are not all the same length. In the first eight episodes of the first season, the total length, including credits, varied between 59:55 (the premiere) and a mere 44:42 (Episode 4). Thus some episodes contain four acts, others three. Initially, *The Sopranos* followed a formula of having one or two strands of the narrative achieve closure within a single episode, while five or six ongoing plotlines proceeded across episodes, some quickly, some slowly: Tony Soprano's visits to a psychiatrist, Dr. Melfi; his wife Carmela's conflicts with their daughter, Meadow; Tony's problems with his pugnacious rival within the gang, Uncle Junior, as well as with his rebellious underling, Chris; his mother Livia's resistance to being put in a nursing home; and Tony's ambivalence about his son's growing recognition of his mob connections. (This formula of multiple plotlines, as we shall see shortly, was pioneered by *Hill Street Blues* and is common in one type of contemporary television drama.) Although not all of these plotlines featured in every episode, the weave was apparently too dense. After four episodes, the program began dealing with fewer separate plotlines per episode, typically having one closure line and significant progress within only two ongoing arcs (although important dangling causes concerning other ongoing lines are dropped in occasionally without immediate development, as when midway through Episode 8, Livia reveals to Uncle Junior that Tony is seeing a psychiatrist).

The Sopranos' act divisions are less obviously marked than those in *Sex and the City*. In the initial four episodes, a series of scenes introduces basic premises in all the lines that will feature in that program. The point at which all the premises are in place I take to be the end of the first act. These premises are developed in parallel until a new set of premises signals the end of the second act, and the last act resolves the closure line and ends with dramatic dangling causes for the ongoing ones (as with Uncle Junior's murder of one of Tony's underlings, Brendan, at the end of Episode 3). Beginning with Episode 5, when the number of lines was reduced, the A plot tends to determine the act breaks. Although the acts are not as even in length as those in programs with commercial breaks would likely be, neither are they wildly out of proportion to each other (see Table 2.3). (The anomalously short fourth act in Episode 6 functions more as a long epilogue than as a climax.) Thus, clearly, a successful cable series like *The Sopranos* has more flexibility than it probably would on one of the networks, and it occasionally takes advantage of the option to include unusually short or lengthy acts.

Such divisions of programs into acts, whether rigidly or flexibly proportioned, are not simply arbitrary. They give an episode a sense of structure, much as the balanced movements of a classical concerto do. They provide the spectator with a sense of progress and guarantee the introduction of dramatic new premises or obstacles at intervals. They allow for the rising and falling action

Table 2.3   Time length of acts in *The Sopranos* episodes

Episode	Act 1	Act 2	Act 3	Act 4
1	11:42	14:50	17:26	13:26
2	16:56	12:21	17:49	
3	14:24	14:01	11:52	
4	15:17	16:30	18:36	
5	11:32	15:00	12:10	15:12
6	13:08	13:15	12:30	8:16
7	15:34	19:19	13:30	
8	14:31	13:58	17:44	

that many writers refer to as crucial to good plots. Regular turning points also give variety to a story, ensuring that the action does not simply involve a character striving toward a goal and meeting a series of similar obstacles. Thus there are reasons why even television episodes that are broadcast without breaks would draw on an act structure.

MULTIPLE STORIES AND STORY ARCS

One type of narrative structure in TV complicates the placement of turning points considerably. There has been a trend in hour-long dramas toward a more dense weave of multiple storylines developing simultaneously. This approach was pioneered by writer/producer Steve Bochco in the much-praised series *Hill Street Blues*, which ran from 1981 to 1987 and essentially established a new format for scripting in many hour-long dramatic series. By late in its run, *Hill Street Blues* had seventeen regular characters. Apparently, however, the series' earliest episodes had tested the limits of what people could absorb in this relatively short time span. A historian of American teleplay writing describes what happened: "The first half-season of *Hill Street*, from January to May 1981, did not get good ratings. NBC, which had low ratings as a network, renewed the show, but with the insistence that there be at least one storyline completed per episode, since the network felt audiences had trouble following storylines wandering through many episodes."[8] This pattern of achieving closure on at least one storyline while continuing others has been increasingly common ever since, as witnessed by such serials as *E.R.* and *The Sopranos* in the States and ITV's *Bad Girls* in the U.K.

The technique of interweaving several important storylines

goes back to soap operas, which have long used this strategy. A modern American hour-long daytime soap opera typically keeps eight to ten stories going at once.[9] The same technique was imported to prime-time television in the U.S. through *Dallas* (1978 to 1991) and *Dynasty* (1981 to 1989). These, in turn, inspired what are sometimes termed "professional dramas," such as *Hill Street Blues, St. Elsewhere, L.A. Law, The West Wing,* and *Boston Central. The Sopranos* creates an ironic variant on this genre.

One teleplay manual claims that since the early 1980s there has also been a trend toward multistory sitcoms: "Each story thread is a main story in its own right, featuring one of the show's lead characters. However, since all of these threads has to be crammed together in a half hour of television, each one incorporates few story beats [i.e., significant causal events] and occupies less screen time than a traditional main story."[10] This struck me as somewhat implausible, so I tested the claim on an episode (January 4, 2001)of the author's main example, *Friends.* This series has six major characters, three men and three women, who are generally given equal weight across the series. The episode I analyzed had three stories, each involving two of the characters; the scenes rotated among them, totaling a mere twenty minutes and twenty-four seconds of actual story time (sans credits and ads). As I expected, the three plotlines were not accorded equal time. One was given distinctly more weight; it was a serious story in which Phoebe is torn between her commitment to have dinner with her friend Joey and her desire to see a long-lost boyfriend who is leaving town that same night. This plotline occupied just under ten minutes, or nearly half the total screen time. A comic plotline about Rachel and Taylor's obsession with cheesecake totals about five and a half minutes, and one about Monica's annoyance at not being invited to her cousin's wedding took just under five minutes. Perhaps these story lines have been made more prominent than the B and C plotlines of traditional sitcoms, but B and C plots they remain. The real difference is that across episodes the major characters take turns at being the center of the A plot—something that is rarer in a sitcom based around one main character. *Sex and the City* similarly moves among the four female friends, but Carrie's plots usually occupy more time than the others.

Nevertheless, multiple story lines, whether in sitcoms or dramas, do give the impression of cramming a great deal of action into a relatively short time span. The same manual on sitcom scripting suggests a reason for this impression that would apply to all multiple-story programs: "The synergistic effect of multiple story threads being woven together gives them as much dramatic power as a traditional sitcom's single main story."[11] This claim seems plausible. In a single episode of *E.R.* or *Bad Girls*, the individual scenes are mostly very short, providing only a slight bit of progression in a given plotline. By moving quickly among plots, the narrative gives the impression of considerable density and "lifelikeness." This is why so many dramatic serials are set in large institutions such as hospitals, police stations, law firms, and prisons, where many characters' concerns can bounce off each other.

This impression of density and realism has also been a factor in the claim by some critics that the introduction of such series has marked a step up in quality from other types of programs. In 1995, Charles McGrath argued that television had entered a golden age—but he added: "I should quickly explain here that by TV I don't mean all TV, or even most of it. I don't mean the tabloid exposés of Sally, Ricki, Geraldo and the rest. I don't mean the sitcoms . . . I don't mean the prime-time soaps . . . And I especially don't mean highbrow TV like 'Masterpiece Theater' . . . The TV shows I have in mind are the weekly network dramatic series."[12] As I suggested in the introduction, I am claiming that in fact the sitcoms and the prime-time (and even daytime) soaps can have complex narrative strategies that are usually hidden. The multiple-story dramas make some of these strategies obvious by their virtuoso juggling of characters and plotlines.

Many of the means by which such programs do that juggling, however, lie firmly within the classical conventions discussed in Chapter 1. The increase in the number of plotlines that interrupt each other has made such dramas concomitantly even more dependent on redundancy, dialogue hooks, appointments, deadlines, and, especially, emphatically marked dangling causes that can carry over several scenes involving other plotlines.[13]

Moreover, series based on multiple plotlines per episode will probably always be far outnumbered by sitcoms with A and B plotlines and by dramas that achieve complete closure. In 2002, *Variety* noted a move toward more old-fashioned plotting in the wake of the collapse of advertising revenues in 2001. Intricately plotted programs might win critical attention, but "critical acclaim has become the kiss of death for many a new show." Dana Walden, copresident of Twentieth Century Fox Television, commented, "It's hard to miss the point that these close-ended episodic dramas and family comedies are very accessible to mass audiences."[14] As I have suggested, however, multiple plots are not the only source of complexity in television narratives.

SERIALITY AND STORY ARCS

There is another reason such programs give the impression of complex overlapping narrative. The multiple-story plot grew up in tandem with a growing emphasis on seriality in prime time.

Originally most sitcoms and dramatic series were made up of self-contained episodes. The outcome of any one episode had no effect on later ones, and it made little difference in what order they were run. There were occasional exceptions, as when midway through the run of *I Love Lucy* in the 1950s, Lucy gave birth to a son who became a regular character. In general, however, sitcom protagonists were considered characters who made some sort of mistake each week, learned a lesson, and promptly forgot it and got into trouble again. Similarly, detectives in dramas solved a case each week, doctors cured a patient, and so on.

During the 1970s, one important sitcom that introduced an element of change was *The Mary Tyler Moore Show* (1970–1977). Although each episode achieved closure for its plotlines, Mary was allowed to mature as a character. The employees of the television station where she worked changed occasionally, got married or promoted, and so on. Mary herself moved from one apartment to another. Other sitcoms have had such occasional changes, though these are usually not sudden or radical enough to prevent the viewer from understanding the action when seeing the series out of order.[15] Still, such story arcs, or threads that continue over more than one episode, present a source of potential complexity in a relatively simple format.[16]

The smaller number of episodes in many British sitcom series offers the possibility of using story arcs across part or all of a run. Take the first season of *The Royle Family* (1998). I tentatively take it to be a sitcom, or at least that hybrid form, a "dramedy."[17] The series is remarkable for having no plotline of longer than about ten minutes within any one of the season's six episodes; nonetheless, Denise's impending wedding, six weeks off in the first episode and about to occur at the end of the last, gives the whole a minimal sense of cohesion.[18]

The case of *Yes, Minister* is more straightforward. In the first
episode, Jim Hacker is characterized as naive and idealistic, and
thus easily defeated by the ultra-cynical bureaucrat Sir Humphrey
Appleby. Individual episodes conform to a simple pattern, with
Jim conceiving a sweeping reform in the first half and Sir
Humphrey scotching it in the second. Jim does, however, gradually become a bit more sophisticated and occasionally gets the
better of Sir Humphrey. In the process, however, he also suc-
cumbs to the temptations of bureaucratic sloth. This story arc is
planted in Episode 2, as Bernard urges Jim to clear his In box by
simply putting everything in the Out box for underlings to handle
(a tactic he had described in an earlier scene):

Jim, standing behind the desk in his office, with Bernard facing him.

JIM, *exasperated:*   "When am I going to do all this correspon-
dence?"

BERNARD: "Well, Minister . . ."

*He glances back and forth between the In and Out boxes. Jack hesitat-
ingly picks up the stack from the In box and, when Bernard nods, he
transfers it to the Out box with a decisive thump.*

BERNARD: "Well done, Minister. Better out than in."

Nothing comes of this exchange immediately, and it becomes a
dangling cause not picked up at all in Episode 3. The pay off
comes in Episode 4, where Jim's wife Annie berates him for becoming a mere government mouthpiece:

*Jim, sitting on the bed in his bedroom talking to Annie. He has just
told her that their anniversary trip to Paris is off. Angry, she starts un-
packing.*

JIM, *trying to change the subject:* "See me on TV tonight?"

ANNIE: "I saw somebody who *looked* like you."

JIM: "What's that supposed to mean?"

ANNIE: "Nothing."

JIM: "Frank Weisel says I've just become a civil-service mouth-piece."

ANNIE: "Yes."

JIM: "What do you mean, 'yes'?"

ANNIE: "Well, *yes.*"

JIM: "You mean you agree?"

ANNIE: "Of course."

JIM: "What do you mean, 'of course'?"

ANNIE: "I mean you could have hired an actor to say it all for you. He'd have said it better. And while you're at it, why not just sign your letters with a rubber stamp or get an assistant principal to sign them for you. They write them anyway."

JIM, *indignantly:* "Assistant principals do not write my letters. Undersecretaries do that."

ANNIE: "I rest my case, m'lud."

In this case a simple parallel is created.

By the second series, *Yes, Prime Minister,* Jim has become so ad-ept at bureaucratic reasoning that he can hold his own in hilarious rapid-fire arguments with the wily Sir Humphrey. Antony Jay, co-author of the two "Minister" series, has discussed the development of Jim Hacker's character: "As Hacker spent more time in government it became impossible for him to continue in the ignorance and naivety that had provided so much scope for comedy when he first arrived [in office] . . . We were compelled to construct more sophisticated errors and traps for him to fall into."[19] Compelled, presumably, because simple techniques that had sufficed for the creation of a short series had to be rendered more complex when the show's success extended its life.

As all of these examples suggest, writers for programs containing story arcs need to plan the plot structure of both the single episode and the ongoing story as well. In the U.S. television market, there is an additional constraint on any type of series: the shape of the season itself. American series tend to involve more episodes than British ones, and they typically fit into a season with a pattern of its own. One writer/producer of television programs has described how a series is planned once a network buys it. The writer/producer who created it becomes a "show runner," the person who runs the series:

> A show runner arcs a season's worth of shows like a writer structures a script. With a season opener, a first-act ending, which is your holiday show that in America would be either a Thanksgiving or a Christmas show; a mid-point two-parter which comes during something called "sweeps week," which is where the advertising agencies set their rates on the basis of the popularity of a show, so you're going to do a really high-concept show during sweeps week; and a season's closer, which is an intriguing development to make sure the audience returns to the show in the fall.[20]

Thus the writing team creating plotlines for a commercial serial program often must shape both the individual episode and the season. They must also assume that their program will go on indefinitely, even though in reality it might be summarily canceled. This conceptual juggling of levels of narrative would seem to be one of the distinctive qualities of storytelling in series television.

The conventions of multiple-story dramas encourage writers to pace the plotlines differently from those of more conventional programs. Typically the self-contained story to be closed off within the episode proceeds at a brisk pace. Action intended to arc over several episodes moves a bit more slowly, and really long-term plotlines add only a tiny bit of information each time they surface. To take an example from the sixth episode of the first series of *Bad Girls*, a combination soap opera and professional drama set in a women's prison, there are three main plotlines in play. One concerns longtime prisoner Dennie, whose alcoholic mother is admitted to the prison; this plotline ends with Dennie reconciling with her mother. The ongoing story of the pregnant addict Zandra's attempts to blackmail the guard Lorna moves a bit more slowly, as this is an ongoing premise. Finally, the relationship between the lesbian prisoner Nikki and the wing governor Helen, which was still developing at the end of the second season, moves forward in tiny increments. Thus scriptwriters must calculate not only how to move between plotlines but also how much causal material to allot to make each fit its intended duration.

REDUNDANCY, OR "DISPERSED EXPOSITION"

Another intriguing aspect of television gets far less attention from teleplay manuals. Given the nature of television viewing, it is highly likely that new viewers will be tuning in at any given moment, both between and during programs. All but the most dedicated viewer is likely to miss an occasional episode of a favorite show. Thus even someone familiar with the central characters, setting, and premises will need occasional filling-in. Other viewers may know the show but begin watching partway through an episode. Still others are completely unfamiliar with the program but tune in and, finding it appealing, begin to watch an episode. Thus a teleplay writer must assume that at any time someone might need information on past events, while others are thoroughly familiar with the show already. The dilemma this poses for the author has been brilliantly described by P. G. Wodehouse, who juggled several long-lived literary series. The fourteen books in the Jeeves and Wooster saga extended over a remarkable sixty years of publishing history. In one of the late entries, Bertie begins, as he often does, by describing Jeeves serving breakfast. After a little over a page, however, he breaks off to muse:

> Well, all right so far. Off to a nice start. But now we come to something which gives me pause. In recording the latest instalment of the Bertram Wooster Story, a task at which I am about to have a pop, I don't see how I can avoid delving into the past a good deal, touching on events which took place in previous instalments, and explaining who's who and what happened when and where and why, and this will make it heavy going for those who have been with me from the start. "Old hat" they will cry or, if French, "Déjà Vu."
>
> On the other hand, I must consider the new customers. I can't just leave the poor perishers to try to puzzle things out for themselves . . .
>
> The only way out that I can think of is to ask the old gang to let their attention wander for a bit—there are heaps of things they can be doing; washing the car, solving the crossword puzzle, taking the dog for a run,—while I place the facts before the newcomer.[21]

Wodehouse has a great advantage: he writes so well that the old gang will not get bored by Bertie's descriptions of past events. Indeed, as this passage indicates, Wodehouse makes humor even out of the necessity of recapitulating past story events.

The same challenge becomes pervasive for teleplay authors. In most cases, the narrative will include what I call "dispersed exposition," a type of redundancy that seems specific to television. As discussed in Chapter 1, films repeatedly present their important information, primarily in order to guarantee that all audience members grasp what is going on. Indeed, for much of cinema history, continuous screenings meant that audience members did not always come in at the beginning of a feature. In crowded big-city cinemas, people lined up outside and were admitted whenever a seat became available—even if the feature was partly over and the viewer would see the end before the beginning. This style of viewing disappeared decades ago, but it undoubtedly helped establish the habit of repetition in film storytelling. Television still must face a similar problem—though one intensified by the fact that the beginning will not roll around again for the latecomer. Thus, although one might intuitively assume that short-form television would need less redundancy than a feature film, it perhaps needs even more.

Self-contained episodes of series, such as sitcoms, would seem on casual observation to require little if any recapping. Yet one manual suggests that the commercial break midway through makes a recap desirable: "When the next act starts, after the break, the new act usually begins by having one of the characters briefly recap what has happened in the story, to reorient viewers."[22] Such recaps are usually not as bald and obvious as this passage makes them sound. To demonstrate this point, let us return to the beginning of the last part of the same *Murphy Brown* episode quoted earlier, in which the title character is pregnant.

Before the commercial break, Murphy and her partner Eldin were attending the first of two weekend Lamaze classes; now we see them at the second. This episode follows a common pattern of sitcoms, where the situation teaches the central character a lesson. In this case, Murphy has a nonchalant attitude toward her impending childbirth, and by the end she will learn that she needs to take the whole process more seriously. Imagine that you have just tuned in during the commercial and know very little, if anything, about this program; note how quickly you are given the basic information you need:

A group of couples in a classroom. The men are massaging their pregnant wives.

ELDIN, *off:*   "Touch relaxation is a way of reducing anxiety. Light stroking of the hair should be done in a gentle, even rhythm . . ."

Pan to reveal Eldin on his knees reading a manual while Murphy lounges on the floor, eating a pastry and reading a newspaper.

ELDIN, *continues reading:*   ". . . to achieve a calming effect."

He eyes Murphy uncertainly, rolls up one sleeve, and begins to stroke her hair awkwardly. She does a slow burn.

MURPHY, *loudly:*   "Eldin, what the hell are you doing?"

ELDIN: "I'm practicing a relaxation technique."

MURPHY: "Well, jeez, why don't you just toss me a biscuit and check my belly for ticks?!"

ELDIN, *sitting beside her:*   "You know, I don't understand this. I'm the only one who's doin' any work here."

MURPHY, *lolling back:*   "Oh, why should I work? Everything they're teaching is just common sense. When the time comes, the baby will be born and that's it."

The cheery female instructor comes in.

INSTRUCTOR: "Sorry for the delay. I was on the phone with Robbie. He and Lisa had their baby."

MURPHY *gets up awkwardly:* "Wait a minute! What do you mean, they had their baby? She's not due until a week after I am."

INSTRUCTOR: "This might be a good time to remind everyone that a due date is just an approximation. The important thing is that Robbie and Lisa came through with flying colors."

MURPHY, *loudly:* "Oh yeah? Let's hear some specifics. How long did it take?"

INSTRUCTOR, *cheerful smile fading a bit:* "Not . . . unusually long for a first baby."

MURPHY: "Well, what does that mean? Ten hours? Fifteen? Twenty?"

INSTRUCTOR: "Thirty-nine."

MURPHY, *appalled, to the others:* "Did you hear that? Thirty-nine hours! That's a bus ride to Boise!"

Both the Lamaze class and Murphy's overly casual attitude are re-established for what Wodehouse calls the "new customers." This passage then goes on to give us our first hint that Murphy is beginning to realize the problems she may face; it leads into the episode's climax. The teacher shows a video of an actual birth, leading Murphy to begin taking her preparations seriously.

Here the recap is delayed slightly by the gag of Eldin stroking Murphy's hair, so that the redundant information comes fairly logically into the scene through their little argument. Integrating such exposition is one of the major skills a scriptwriter must possess. The challenge is perhaps greatest in American soap operas, where several storylines progress daily. In fact, the average American soap-opera viewer in the 1990s watched only two and a half episodes a week, meaning that he or she missed fully half of the story action. Magazines exist solely to give plot synopses of all the network soap operas, so clearly viewers do care about keeping up with the story. Still, the network executives prefer that people watch their programs and advertisements, and one way of attracting them is to ensure that they can easily grasp the story when they do tune in. A manual on scripting for soap operas contains the most extensive discussion of recapping that I have found:

> Recap is fraught with hazards. If it is used at all, it must be used in a normal, believable, and dramatically justifiable manner . . . If it is not handled skillfully, if it is not integrated into the dramatic essence of the scene, it will stick out like a sore thumb and is one of the factors that made old-fashioned soap writing so deplorable . . .
>
> I can't think of any infallible rules for writing good recap, but there is a rule about bad recap. If so much as one line of dialogue calls attention to itself as recap, out with it! If our writer finds she can't incorporate the necessary information into the fabric of the scene so that its very utterance sounds as impulsive as all the rest of the dialogue, she shouldn't recap at all. That, in fact, seems to be the trend in today's soaps . . . Let the viewers figure out what's going on, or let them tune in more often![23]

The writer, however, cannot ensure that viewers will watch regularly and attentively, so recapping remains a necessity.

A fairly successful example occurs in the fifth episode of the first season of *Bad Girls*. This scene occurs just after what I take to be a midway commercial break.[24] There has been a gap of time since the previous action, a night having passed. The guards and Helen, the female wing governor, have their morning meeting. Within a minute, all three of the episode's major plotlines are mentioned: the young guard Dominic's desire to quit, the recent suicide of a prisoner named Rachel, and Helen's decision to transfer an unruly prisoner, Nikki, out of solitary confinement:

High angle extreme long shot of the prison, with a truck pulling up in the yard. Cut to the guards' lounge. Dominic enters and sits, with Jim in the background. Jim turns the tabloid paper he is reading to display a female nude.

JIM: "Glamour photographer?"

DOMINIC: "There's no need to take [inaudible]"

JIM: "Just taking a friendly interest in your alternative career plans. Look, if you want to throw away decent money and a good pension, that's up to you, mate."

DOMINIC: "Felt like throwin' up coming in this morning."

HELEN, *bustling in:* "OK, we've got a lot to get through. Right! Investigation into Rachel's death."

JIM, *stern:* "Before we go on, Helen, I'd like to raise the matter of Nikki Wade. She assaulted a fellow prisoner. Now she's back on the wing. Why?"

HELEN, *defiant:* "Because I said so!"

JIM: "Well, excuse me, but we're professionals, trying to do a professional day's work. We can't do that if the good order of the prison's gonna be disrupted by troublemakers like Wade."

FEMALE GUARD: "I agree!"

HELEN: "I made a deal with Nikki."

JIM: "Oh. So, what, we're negotiating with 'em now, are we?"

HELEN: "Look, Jim, you said yourself, Nikki Wade is one of the most difficult prisoners you've had to deal with. I'm trying a different tack—treating her like a human being and trusting her."

FEMALE GUARD: "Well, excuse me, Mum. It's all very well for you to say you trust Wade—but *we're* the ones at the cell door. *We've* got to take the abuse and the assaults, not you."

DOMINIC: "I think we should give it a try. Maybe it'll work. Let's face it, nothing else has."

Not only do we grasp a bit of what's going on, but the antagonisms and alliances among the group are quickly laid out. *Bad Girls*, though a British series, is constructed very much in the American style, rapidly shifting among many short scenes. It also demonstrates how to repeat a great deal of story information without the process being particularly obvious. As in this case and in the *Murphy Brown* scene described earlier, having the characters get into an argument provides an excuse for them to refer in a natural way to familiar facts.

I do not wish to imply that all redundancy in television storytelling functions to fill in on past material for newcomers. Just as in films, important narrative information may be planted repeat-

edly to guarantee our understanding. Such planting occurs in one
of the best of the *Fawlty Towers* episodes, "Basil the Rat."[25] As you
no doubt recall, the episode hinges on a pet rat that Mañuel has
been ordered to get rid of but which he has secretly hidden in a
shed just as the health inspector is about to pay a visit. Basil
Fawlty puts rat poison on a piece of veal, which then gets mixed
up with the rest of the meat for that day's lunch special. The re-
mainder of the plot hinges on whether the hotel cat becomes ill
after nibbling a particular piece of the veal. This cat has not figured in previous episodes, so it is established in no fewer than
three scenes before its crucial action of eating the veal:

FIRST SCENE: the kitchen

SYBIL, *to Basil:*   "See how many fire extinguishers are missing."
He exits, she dons a plastic smock.

SYBIL: "Come on, Polly, we'll start here."

POLLY, *to black cat on floor:*   "Not in here, Puss." *She makes a chir-
ruping noise with her lips, picks it up, and puts it out the back door.*

SECOND SCENE: the kitchen

Sybil, Polly, and Terry are cleaning the room.

SYBIL: ". . . doing the walls, Terry, the filters, check the fridges,
aah . . ." *She spots the cat and carries it to the back door.*

BASIL, *entering:* "Right, that's done."

THIRD SCENE: the area outside the kitchen door. Mañuel
emerges with a saucer of food and cup of water, furtively looking
around. Another shot shows the sidewalk and a nearby shed, with

the same cat in front of the door; it yowls as Mañuel approaches. He chases it away with a kicking gesture and begins to open the shed door.

FOURTH SCENE: the kitchen

Terry is in the kitchen, working. Basil enters.

BASIL: "All right, Terry, everything under control?"

TERRY: "Yeah, is he [the inspector] still . . .?"

BASIL: "No, he started upstairs. God knows where that rat is. Oh, Puss!" *He runs to the cat, which is nibbling at veal in a pan; it yowls when he picks it up.*

BASIL: "Oh, come on, Puss," *and puts it out the door.*

Such planting of important information recalls very similar strategies in nearly every narrative art form. Exposition is a fundamental principle of storytelling, but it takes a distinctive form in series television.

I hope I have given you a sense of where some of the complexity of television narrative lies. As in classical Hollywood filmmaking, the mechanics of storytelling are not meant to be noticeable. Instead, the spectator should be able to comprehend the story easily enough that the experience of viewing remains entertaining.

This hidden complexity also suggests another reason why so little formal analysis of television has been done. Certain questions that the analyst might wish to investigate would probably necessitate looking not just at individual programs, but at seasons as well, and ideally entire runs.[26] In many cases this would be a daunting project, especially considering the challenge of finding complete sets of long-running shows. Still, these ideas about story arcs and dispersed exposition may suggest some ways of looking at a few of the distinctive and intriguing aesthetic aspects of narrative television.

3

THE DISPERSAL OF NARRATIVE:

ADAPTATIONS, SEQUELS, SERIALS,

SPIN-OFFS, AND SAGAS

ADAPTATION STUDIES

This chapter begins with the question of adaptations of narratives, specifically those from television into film and film into television. By suggesting a few reasons why adaptations are made and examining some examples, I spin out several more general ideas about the roles the two media have played in the narrative arts of the late twentieth and early twenty-first centuries.

The idea of studying adaptations may seem a bit odd to those used to exploring the more traditional arts. It goes back to the early days of academic film studies from the 1950s to the early 1970s. Classes dealing with adaptations explored the nature of filmic art by comparing it with literature. Such an approach was a way of bringing film, which had not really gained wide acceptance within academia, into the classroom. Today, comparing film to literature is not an approach commonly used in film-studies departments in universities. It does flourish in many foreign-language departments, which find that more students are attracted to a course in, say, Spanish literature and film than to one in Spanish literature alone.

In film-studies courses, the classic texts are seldom those dealing with adaptation. Perhaps the main exception is a pair of essays on the relationship of cinema to theater and to novels by the great film theorist André Bazin. Even in this case, I suspect that these essays are read mainly because they are anthologized as part of his important work *What Is Cinema?* and because they deal with classic films like Olivier's *Henry V.*[1] They do tell us something about the nature of cinema, and they add nuance to Bazin's theory as a whole. Few analysts as insightful as Bazin, however, have tackled this issue.

On the whole, adaptation studies have pointed out traits of cinema that seem obvious. Plays supposedly need to be "opened out" in order to use the spatial freedom provided by the film camera. (Bazin argues against opening out plays, opining that film should respect theatricality—a contrary position that gives his essay part of its interest.) Novels are difficult to adapt into movies because they tend to be much longer than a commercial film, and even mainstream popular novels often have more complicated plots and characters than a film can handle. For example, when screenwriter Ted Tally adapted Thomas Harris's novel *The Silence of the Lambs* as a film, he reduced its considerable length in part by eliminating two major subplots. One of these involved the death of Jack Crawford's wife; the other dealt with the fact that Clarice Starling risked missing or flunking the FBI special-agent exams by devoting herself to solving the kidnapping. The result of this trimming was a masterful screenplay that used the remaining plotlines to achieve suspense and subtlety of characterization without a sense of rushing through the action.[2] Whether studying such adaptations from literature tells us much about the nature of cinematic art is, however, debatable.[3]

Adaptations between film and television are more intriguing, and not just because the two media share so many techniques. Such transfers of story material form part of a larger pattern that includes sequels, serials, spin-offs, and sagas—other trends that have burgeoned in recent decades. The circulation of plots among media reflects, I would argue, an important change in our conception of narrative itself—and specifically a loosening of the notion of closure and the self-contained work of fictional art. That change has been due, in large part, to television.

WHY ADAPTATIONS ARE INEVITABLE

When the issue of adaptation arises—especially adaptation from film to television or television to film—many viewers' reaction is likely to be one of puzzlement. Why take a narrative conceived in one medium and attempt to transfer it to another? If we assume that each medium has its own constraints and expressive possibilities, then artists must change an existing narrative significantly in appropriating it for a new work in a different medium. In cases where one artwork has told a story well, experience has taught us that the adapted artwork seldom equals or betters the original.

Adaptations of classic works of literature are obviously quite common. Admirers of the original works become defensive and suspicious on hearing that a film or television adaptation is under way. Inevitably reviewers and other commentators compare the new work with the original, usually to the detriment of the new one. This protective sort of scrutiny is currently going on in relation to the three-film version of *The Lord of the Rings* (2001, 2002, 2003). The Internet and fan magazines have generated a seemingly endless debate on the appropriateness of the casting, the setting, and any other details that have become public. (Much of this debate has been encouraged and exploited by the companies involved in the film's production and publicity.) I should add that this kind of scrutiny is applied less to adaptations of contemporary best-sellers like those by Michael Crichton or John Grisham—perhaps partly because such books are so evidently written with the movie adaptation in mind.

There is also still a widespread notion that film, although an art form of sorts, is not as high or pure a form as literature. Many intellectuals would see an adaptation of a great novel or play as an inevitable sullying of the original—despite the common counterclaims that at least such adaptations bring the work to people who never would have read the originals anyway and that sales of the adapted literary works inevitably rise after a film adaptation.

Despite all the doubts and obstacles, however, film and television artists persist in creating works adapted from an enormous range of narrative sources, from opera to comic books. Given the uphill struggle they may face to gain public acceptance, why do they persist? Why not just use original screenplays and teleplays?

The most obvious answer is that producers of expensive artworks like films and television programs hope to guarantee their profitability by exploiting a familiar work. These works have either stood the test of time, as with classics, or made a great deal of money already, in the case of best-sellers. These factors of familiarity and built-in popularity weigh with people who undertake adaptations.

There is another perhaps less obvious factor that I think is at least equally important, and it relates to the sheer quantity of narrative material necessary for today's media. In Chapter 1 I criticized Raymond Williams's concept of "flow" as a way of looking at the aesthetic aspects of television. Williams, however, makes one observation in his book on television that I find very suggestive. He points out that television has made more drama available to audiences than either theatre or film had previously. In this context, Williams is using "drama" to designate not only television broadcasts of theatrical plays but also all fictional programs written directly for the small screen. His description, written in the 1970s, is worth quoting at length:

> There has never been a time, until the last fifty years, when a majority of the population had regular and constant access to drama, and used this access . . . It seems probably that in societies like Britain and the United States more drama is watched in a week or weekend, by the majority of viewers, than would have been watched in a year or in some cases a lifetime in any previous historical period . . . It is clearly one of the unique characteristics of advanced industrial societies that drama as an experience is now an intrinsic part of everyday life, at a quantitative level which is so very much greater than any precedent as to seem a fundamental qualitative change. Whatever the social and cultural reasons may finally be, it is clear that watching dramatic simulation of a wide range of experiences is now an essential part of our modern cultural pattern.[4]

Williams sees the main importance of this proliferation of drama in people's lives primarily in terms of its cultural effects. As I suggested in Chapter 1, the cultural-studies approach has been highly influential in television studies, and it hardly needs any help from me. There are, however, two other implications of the phenomenon, which Williams does not discuss but which intrigue me.

First, I simply want to note in passing that there is the issue of people's enhanced ability to comprehend performed narratives through much more frequent exposure. Before technological developments rendered the recording of theatrical performances possible, audiences outside the cities had very limited access to drama. That access was confined to the occasional touring company and to local plays put on by school or church groups. Film, radio, and television have exponentially increased people's exposure to enacted narratives.[5] Audiences have learned a wide range of genres and forms, and presumably many are able to follow relatively complicated stories told in moving images. Such familiarity may account for the increase in multistory television series, as well as the development of the multimedia saga, such as the many interlinked *Star Trek* tales told in television, film, print, and the Internet.[6] It seems plausible that as people exercise skills of narrative comprehension, they expand their powers of grasping and appreciating such complex stories. In short, at least some spectators may have become fairly sophisticated consumers of narrative.

A second and more immediately pertinent point is that the explosion of mass media outlets has created an insatiable demand for stories of all types. In the nineteenth century, the spread of literacy led to the growth of popular fiction magazines and dime novels, and although the fiction magazines waned in the middle of the twentieth century, they were largely replaced by the mass-market paperback novels that are still very much with us. From the start, these changes encouraged the rise of the freelance writer. Many such writers then started also writing for the movies, which around 1905 adopted fictional narratives as their dominant mode. Radio, comic books, and television increased the market for stories, and the Internet can only accelerate this trend.

Throughout the twentieth century, the common cry of film and television producers has been that there are not enough good stories available. In 1917 the head of the largest French production company, Charles Pathé, wrote at length about the "scenario crisis" as the main factor holding his national film industry back.[7] During the early 1920s, the big and recently formed Hollywood studios sent special representatives to Europe. Their main job was to scout for promising plays and other literary properties that could be bought for adaptation purposes. Sometimes their authors were also signed up for a stretch of lucrative screenwriting in sunny Hollywood.

Even today, the hunger for stories or merely for promising ideas for stories has led to a considerable willingness by both film and television producers to encourage freelance submissions. One might expect that big agents and producers would have little patience with the aspiring, inexperienced writer. Yet in fact producers and their representatives often give out their addresses, and virtually all scripts that are sent in are at least given a quick scan. Of course the vast bulk of these freelance scripts are rejected immediately. Some are optioned, but most of those are never produced. In both film and television, only a tiny number of submitted scripts make it to the screen. Nevertheless, studios cannot risk letting that one great sceenplay get away. Not only would they lose out on a hit movie, but the script might be discovered by a rival firm. A similar openness to freelancers exists in television. Typically a series will have at least three staff writers. If that series runs for several seasons, the staff may find their invention flagging, and they may move on to another show. Replacements may come from the ranks of freelancers who have submitted promising scripts for that particular series.

Legion though they are, contract writers and freelancers must struggle to generate enough stories to fill the large and small screens of the world. Hence the practice of "recycling" narratives through adaptations.

Aside from the fact that the expanding media market needs to be supplied with huge amounts of narrative, individual studios have other important incentives to generate a great many films and television programs. Each year in the U.S. alone, the major firms release 200 to 400 films every year, most of which fail financially. And each year the studios declare that they will cut back the budgets of films and make fewer of them. This claim is nothing new. In the late 1920s the slogan was "fewer but better films," and it was not adhered to then either. From the 1920s through the 1940s, the major U.S. studios owned their own theatre chains, and their output was guaranteed a market. The studio's assets lay in its real estate holdings, including a large filmmaking facility, and the large numbers of stars and behind-the-camera workers under long-term contract. The films themselves, once they had gone through their various runs internationally, were usually considered to have little residual value.

The situation has nearly reversed itself in recent decades. As a result of the Divorcement Decrees in the late 1940s, the big American production-distribution firms have sold off many of their filmmaking facilities. The stars and filmmakers are hired on a film-by-film basis. Now, with the burgeoning media market, the big firms often find that their libraries of older films are their most valuable assets. When Ted Turner bought MGM/UA in 1986, for example, he did not do so with the idea of producing films under that company's banner. His goal was to acquire the vast holdings of old films for his cable stations, TNT and later Turner Classic Movies.[8]

Currently all the familiar studios of Hollywood's golden age are subsidiaries of large multinational corporations.[9] In many cases, adaptations are attractive because such companies already own the rights to various narratives that have already been produced in one medium but which are available to be recycled in another.[10]

Moreover, these huge companies have been able to market their products, including movies, in part by using synergy. That is, a company's TV stations will promote its movies, while its record division puts out the soundtrack, and so on. Such marketing now has also come to mean selling the same narrative over and over in different media. A film released theatrically goes through a series of incarnations: VHS tape, DVD, airplane video, network television broadcast, pay-per-view, and rerun on local television and cable.[11] With the possibility of delivery of video-on-demand through the Internet, yet another way of marketing films looms on the horizon. Cable and satellite transmissions have expanded the television market enormously. Typically network series make a profit only when they are released through syndication, and the value of old programs that sat on the shelf, unseen for decades, has risen.[12] Even the BBC, technically supported by license fees, has a video sales wing that revives older programs like its adaptations of three John LeCarré novels.

The expansion of home video of various sorts has meant that a great many old films and television programs are now available. When I was a graduate student in the 1970s, the possibility of seeing some of Mary Pickford's most famous silent features was virtually nil. Now several of them are out on DVD. Similarly, silent films show up regularly on Turner Classic Movies. Old films are being restored now, not through a sudden awakening of a sense of historical duty in studio executives but because for the first time in many decades those old films have potential monetary worth.

In the midst of all this activity, adapting films into television series and adapting television series into films are small pieces in the overall puzzle. Given the great demand for narratives, however, I suspect that this practice, along with remaking films and creating sequels, is here to stay. So, let us turn to some examples and see what we can learn from them about the recycling and expansion of existing narratives.

ADAPTATIONS: TWO EXAMPLES

Films have been turned into TV shows since at least 1949. Table 3.1 presents a list of such shows, which covers only 1980 to 1998 but should be enough for our purposes.[13] I suspect most of you, like me, have not been aware that some of these shows existed, though many of the titles are familiar from their original cinematic incarnations. Few of these series have had the enormous success that several films adapted from TV shows have enjoyed in the past decade. Nevertheless, hope seems to spring eternal among television producers.[14] It is interesting to note that the rise of cable television may be encouraging a trend toward adaptations. There seems to be a trend toward new series in the science-fiction genre in particular, bolstered by such nonadapted series as *Babylon 5* and the various descendents of the original *Star Trek*. This trend, if it is a trend, may be a response to the immense demand for narrative material by modern media systems, as discussed earlier.[15]

My main example of a film-to-television adaptation is *Buffy the Vampire Slayer*. I believe that *Buffy* is the only network series on my list still running, and it displays no sign of losing its popularity; indeed, it has inspired a successful spin-off, *Angel*. Devoted fans are aware that *Buffy the Vampire Slayer* is based on a 1992 film of the same name, but more casual viewers will no doubt be surprised to learn that there was such a film. It was not a hit, but the

Table 3.1   Television shows adapted from films

1980	*Beyond Westworld, Breaking Away, Freebie and the Bean, Semi-Tough*
1981	*Flamingo Road, Foul Play, Harper Valley P.T.A., Private Benjamin, Walking Tall*
1982	*Fame, Herbie, The Love Bug, 9 to 5, Seven Brides for Seven Brothers*
1983	*Gun Shy [The Apple Dumpling Gang], Hotel*
1984	*Blue Thunder, The Four Seasons*
1985	*Mr. Belvedere, Stir Crazy*
1986	*Fast Times [Fast Times at Ridgemont High], Gung Ho, Starman*
1987	**Bustin' Loose, Nothing in Common, Down and Out in Beverly Hills, *You Can't Take It with You*
1988	*Freddy's Nightmares [Nightmare on Elm Street], In the Heat of the Night, Baby Boom, Dirty Dancing, Dirty Dozen: The Series, *War of the Worlds*
1989	*Alien Nation*
1990	*Adventures of the Black Stallion, Bagdad Cafe, Ferris Bueller, The Outsiders, Parenthood, Swamp Thing, Uncle Buck, Working Girl*
1991	*Baby Talk [Look Who's Talking], Eddie Dodd [True Believer]*
1992	*Bill and Ted's Excellent Adventure, *Highlander, *The Untouchables, The Young Indiana Jones Chronicles*
1993	*A League of Their Own, Problem Child, Snowy River: The McGregor Saga [The Man from Snowy River]*
1994	**RoboCop: The Series, Weird Science*
1995	John Grisham's *The Client*
1996	*The Big Easy, Clueless, Dangerous Minds, *FX: The Series [F/X], Party Girl, What's Happening!! [Cooley High]*
1997	*Buffy the Vampire Slayer, *Conan: The Television Series, *Disney's Honey, I Shrunk the Kids, La Femme Nikita, *Police Academy: The Series, Stargate SG-1, Timecop*
1998	**The Crow: Stairway to Heaven, The Magnificent Seven: The Series, *Mortal Kombat: Conquest, The Net*

Note: Where the title has been changed significantly, the original is given in brackets; asterisks indicate original syndicated programs.

TV series it inspired must rank among the most successful adaptations. (The most successful so far remains *M*A*S*H*.)

Table 3.2 gives a list of films adapted from television shows, the latest being the hit film of *Charlie's Angels*.[16] The list is longer than one might expect, comprising just over eighty titles, and the earliest adapted films date back surprisingly far. Most, of course, are films from American television programs, though a few British ones figure on the list as well: *Bean, Doctor Who, Pennies from Heaven*, and one of my main examples in this chapter, *The Avengers*.

Despite the rather poor reputation of such adaptations, in the decade from 1979 to 1989, the majority of such films made the annual list of the ten top-grossing films: *Star Trek—The Motion Picture* (no. 6 in 1979), *The Blues Brothers* (no. 8 in 1980), *Star Trek II: The Wrath of Khan* (no. 7 in 1982), *Star Trek III: The Search for Spock* (no. 7 in 1984), *Star Trek IV: The Voyage Home* (no. 4 in 1986), *The Untouchables* (no. 5 in 1987), *Dragnet* (no. 8 in 1987), and *Batman* (no. 1 in 1989). (Clearly a large part this success lies in the popularity of the *Star Trek* series—perhaps *the* model of an open-ended, constantly regenerating multimedia narrative.)

Perhaps this series of hits, capped by *Batman*'s enormous success, contributed to the studios' move into TV adaptations as a more regular part of their product in the 1990s. Although some of these films met with disaster (e.g., *It's Pat*), enough have succeeded to guarantee that this particular type of adaptation will not disappear. Together *Mission Impossible* and *Mission Impossible 2* grossed just under a billion dollars worldwide, not counting video and other ancillary markets. *The Fugitive, The Flintstones, Bean*, and *Wild, Wild West* have all grossed over $200 million. The most recent adaptation, *Charlie's Angels*, is still in release and has already grossed around $240 million.[17] Other films on the list have

Table 3.2   Films adapted from television shows

1956	*Our Miss Brooks*
1958	*The Crawling Eye* (British, based on British series, *The Trollenberg Terror*)
1964	*McHale's Navy*
1965	*McHale's Navy Joins the Air Force, Dr. Who and the Daleks* (British)
1977	*Wackiest Wagon Train in the West* (from *Dusty's Trail*)
1979	*Star Trek—The Motion Picture*
1980	*The Nude Bomb* (aka *The Return of Maxwell Smart*), **The Blues Brothers*
1981	*Pennies from Heaven*
1982	*Star Trek II: The Wrath of Khan*
1984	*Star Trek III: The Search for Spock*
1985	*Pee-Wee's Big Adventure*
1986	*Star Trek IV: The Voyage Home*
1987	*Dragnet, The Untouchables*
1988	*The Naked Gun: From the Files of Police Squad*
1989	*Batman, Star Trek V: The Final Frontier*
1990	*Jetsons: The Movie*
1991	*The Addams Family, Naked Gun 2½: The Smell of Fear, Star Trek VI: The Undiscovered Country*
1992	*Batman Returns, Twin Peaks: Fire Walk with Me,* **Wayne's World*
1993	*Addams Family Values, Batman: Mark of the Phantasm, The Beverly Hillbillies,* **Coneheads, Dennis the Menace, The Fugitive, Thunder in Paradise* (TV pilot released theatrically), **Wayne's World 2*
1994	*Alien Nation: Dark Horizon* (based on a series which was based on the film *Alien Nation*), *Car 54, Where Are You? The Flintstones,* **It's Pat, Lassie, Maverick, Naked Gun 33 1/3: The Final Insult, Star Trek: Generations, Thunder in Paradise 2, Thunder in Paradise 3*
1995	*Batman Forever, Baywatch—The Movie: Forbidden Paradise, The Brady Bunch Movie, Phantom 2040 Movie: The Ghost Who Walks,* **Stuart Saves His Family, Tales from the Crypt Presents Demon Knight*
1996	*Beavis and Butt-Head Do America, Kids in the Hall: Brain Candy, Mission: Impossible, Mystery Science Theater 3000: The Movie, Sgt. Bilko, A Very Brady Sequel*
1997	*Batman and Robin, Bean* (British), *George of the Jungle, Good Burger, Leave It to Beaver, McHale's Navy*
1998	*The Avengers,* **Blues Brothers 2000, Lost in Space, A Night at the Roxbury, Pokémon: The First Movie* (Japanese), *The Rugrats Movie, The X-Files*
1999	*Dudley Do-Right, The Flintstones in Viva Rock Vegas, The Mod Squad, My Favorite Martian, South Park: Bigger, Longer, and Uncut,* **Superstar, Wild Wild West*
2000	*The Adventures of Rocky and Bullwinkle, Mission: Impossible 2, Charlie's Angels*

Note: Asterisks indicate films derived from *Saturday Night Live* skits.

been more modest hits: *The Addams Family*, *The Brady Bunch Movie*, *Maverick*, and *The Untouchables*.

My main example of a television-to-film adaptation does not figure on the lists of box-office champions. Quite the contrary: the 1998 film version of *The Avengers* was what could politely be called a financial disappointment. Nevertheless, the original series seemed a logical choice for transfer to film. In the cases of both *Buffy* and *The Avengers*, the TV show distinctly outshines its filmic counterpart (so, although I'm a film scholar, I cannot be accused of bias). These two adaptations have one advantage for purposes of comparison. Both mix comedy with a more serious genre: in the case of *Buffy*, horror and high-school comedy; in *The Avengers*, science fiction and sophisticated comedy.

The different versions of *The Avengers* and *Buffy the Vampire Slayer* point out the growing need for generating more and more narrative material. In each case the adaptation, created several years after the original, reflects the greater use of both *seriality* and *sequels* in both media. *The Avengers*, which was originally composed of individual, self-contained narratives, was made into a film that clearly left the way open for a sequel—a forlorn hope on the part of the producers, as it turned out. Conversely, *Buffy* in its film version was also a self-contained story that achieved a considerable degree of closure at the end. Indeed, the premise that a high school girl has the power to kill vampires would seem to imply that any television series based on it would yield a pretty repetitious set of stories. Yet the television adaptation has been praised as highly inventive in working variations on this somewhat unpromising basis.

The original film has quite a simple plot. A superficial California high school cheerleader is approached by a mysterious man named Merrick. He tells her that she is the Slayer, a woman born each generation who has the power to kill vampires—a group of which happen to be terrorizing the neighborhood. As Merrick trains Buffy for her calling, she starts a tentative romance with a young drifter named Pike. As the battles with the vampires commence, Merrick is killed. Buffy, aided by Pike, defeats the vampires during an attack on the high school dance. In the epilogue, the pair ride off on Pike's motorcycle into an unknown future:

High school gym with students slowly exiting amid the remnants of destroyed decorations. Pike sits groggily on the floor, with Buffy squatting over him, straddling his legs.

BUFFY: "Are you OK?"

PIKE: I can't move my legs . . . cause you're sittin' on 'em."

They laugh, she moves aside and helps him up.

BUFFY: "Ok, come on . . . help ya." *He shrugs off her assistance, painfully gets up, and looks around.*

PIKE: "Did I do all that?"

BUFFY: "No."

PIKE: "Did you do all that?"

BUFFY, *quietly:*   "Yeah, I did."

They walk slowly across the dance floor.

PIKE: "I, uh, I saved you a dance." *Pause.*

BUFFY, *uncertainly:*   "You gonna ask me?"

He puts an arm around her waist and they begin to dance.

PIKE: "I suppose you wanna lead."

BUFFY: "No."

PIKE: "Me neither."

BUFFY: "This is a good thing."

They dance slowly to the sound of a distant siren. Rock music swells. They embrace and dance.

Dissolve to close-up of a hand starting a motorcycle engine. Song, "Close Our Eyes and Dream" begins as Buffy climbs on the cycle behind Pike and they roar into the distance.

The film makes little attempt to start a narrative that could sustain a sequel. As Buffy learns the craft of vampire slaying, she becomes more serious and gives up her friendships with various shallow schoolmates, virtually cutting herself off from the social life of the school. Her rich, uncaring parents leave her to do whatever she wants and hence provide no narrative tension. Merrick's sudden death about two-thirds of the way through the film cuts off much of the narrative's impetus. The film's main interest is summed up by its title, with its blend of fluffy comedy and horror. This mixture is worked out in a charming and amusing way in the scenes between Merrick, played by Donald Sutherland, and Buffy. He takes her perfectly seriously and treats her with gallant deference even when she defies or insults him in Valley Girl slang. Once Merrick is dead, the later scenes follow a conventional low-budget teenage-horror-film plot. By the end, Buffy has only Pike, since both her friends and parents offer no potential life commensurate with her newfound powers.

The TV series opens with a two-episode narrative that changes many of the film's premises in order to create the potential for narrative variety in a long-running series. The film's writer, Joss

Whedon, also scripted the opening episodes (as well as many of the subsequent ones). *Buffy* the series has a complicated relation to *Buffy* the movie. It is ostensibly a sequel, since at the beginning of the first episode Buffy already knows that she is a vampire slayer. She has come to a new town and high school because she was expelled from her old school for burning down the gymnasium—in order to kill vampires, as she explains. In fact in the film Buffy had not burned down the gym in disposing of the vampires. Possibly this reference is an homage to Brian De Palma's *Carrie* (1976), a film mixing teenage drama and gothic horror, which may have been an inspiration for Whedon in creating *Buffy*.

Although technically a sequel, the opening two episodes of the TV series constitute a sort of remake of the film as well, in that the plot is nearly parallel to that of the original. Buffy again meets a mentor figure, encounters a snobbish, gossipy popular girl, fights a gang of vampires that live in an underground cavern, and finally defeats them at a dance, in this case at a local club. Whedon has, however, taken the opportunity to change several of the plot premises so as to provide more potential for indefinitely generating a variety of narratives.

Buffy's uncaring mother and father from the movie are replaced by a concerned mother. The latter remains remarkably oblivious to her daughter's extracurricular activities hunting monsters, but she at least tries to make her do her homework—thus generating some obstacles to Buffy's carrying out her duties. Buffy also gains a set of friends among the unpopular crowd at the high school—an element largely missing from the film. These friends can act as helpers to Buffy, as when Willow, the mousy computer geek, finds information on the Internet—a quick way of motivating the characters' rapid acquisition of any specialized knowledge they may need during a plot. The character of Merrick in the film, a mysterious, dignified figure, is replaced by Giles, the school librarian. He seems somehow to know about Buffy's powers from the moment she arrives at school, but he himself has no special powers and acts more as a comic, fallible guide to Buffy, constantly trying to keep her focused on her duties despite her longing for a social life.

And then there is the mouth of Hell, above which Buffy's new high school happens to be built. Presumably fate drew her to this spot, where not only vampires but all sorts of other demons periodically erupt into the mundane world of Sunnydale. Despite the series' title, Buffy turns out to be capable of fighting any sort of monster. Given this larger number of characters and far broader premise concerning supernatural foes, there are considerably wider possibilities for plot generation than in the film. This new premise is made explicit by Giles at the end of the two-part opener, as Buffy and her new friends chatter on in normal teenage fashion:

Buffy, who sucks on a lollipop through this scene, meets Xander in the courtyard of the high school.

BUFFY: "What exactly were you expecting?"

XANDER: "I don't know, something. I mean, the dead rose. We should've at least had an assembly."

Giles and Willow join them.

GILES: "People have a tendency to rationalize what they can and forget what they can't."

BUFFY, *agreeing:* "Believe me, I've seen it happen."

WILLOW: "Well, *I'll* never forget it. None of it."

GILES: "Good. Next time you'll be prepared."

XANDER: "Next time?"

WILLOW: "Next time is why?"

GILES: "Well, we prevented the Master from freeing himself and opening the mouth of Hell. That's not to say he's going to stop trying. I'd say the fun is just beginning."

WILLOW: "*More* vampires?"

GILES: "Not just vampires. The next threat we face may be something quiet different."

BUFFY, *shrugging:*   "*I* can hardly wait."

GILES: "We're at the center of a mystical convergence here. We may in fact stand between the Earth and its total destruction."

BUFFY: "Well, I gotta look on the bright side. Maybe I can still get kicked out of school." *She, Willow, and Xander walk on, chatting.*

XANDER: "Oh, yeah, that's a plan. 'Cause lots of schools are not Hellmouths."

WILLOW: "Maybe you could blow something up. They're really strict about that."

BUFFY: "I was thinking of a more subtle approach, you know? Like excessive not-studying."

GILES *moves into the foreground, watching them and then turning front:* "The Earth is doomed." *He exits.*

Oddly enough, the TV series also seems to have a larger budget for special effects than the film had, or at least a more imaginative design staff, and the TV monsters are often more visually impressive and threatening than the rather ineffectual vampires of the original.

The series also takes advantage of the more complicated narrative strategies offered by series television. Many of the episodes use self-contained plotlines about monsters that play out to closure by the end. There are also, however, ongoing storylines that develop gradually, as with Buffy's lengthy romantic entanglement with a "good" vampire named Angel. This mixture of closed and open storylines never becomes as elaborate as the multiple-story dramas of the *Hill Street Blues* variety. Nevertheless, the element of seriality has helped to give the series a surprisingly long life.

The film version of *The Avengers* is essentially a remake of, or even prequel to, the Emma Peel portion of the series rather than being in any way a sequel. (The Peel episodes constitute seasons four and five of the original, though they were the first ones shown on American television.) The film starts earlier in the story than the series does by having Peel and Steed meet for the first time. In the series, they have obviously known each other for some time by Peel's first appearance. She is a scientist, but her speciality is left deliberately vague so that she can supply any sort of technical knowledge. Steed is a government secret agent, and Peel assists him on some quasi-official basis. All indications are that they are already lovers at the point where we first meet Peel.

The film feels distinctly like an expanded typical episode of the TV series, in that it is based on a single plotline consisting of a villain who uses an odd invention in an attempt to dominate the world. The main villain, played by Sean Connery, devises a machine to control the world's weather. His plan is to blackmail every country into paying him a huge sum—in effect buying good weather from him.

In fact the plot and certain motifs and individual scenes are a patchwork of borrowings from various episodes of the original series. The weather-controlling machine comes from "A Surfeit of H_2O," the invisible man who works at the Ministry derives from "The See-Through Man," and the scene in which Peel runs through the same corridors over and over derives from "The House that Jack Built." I'm sure there are many other specific borrowings that aficionados could catch. The odd thing is that the writers seem quite familiar with the series and yet have completely failed to capture its original appeal.[18]

Ironically, the TV version of *The Avengers* achieves greater closure than does the film. Most of the episodes in the Diana Rigg seasons are self-contained narratives that could be viewed in any order. The exception is the first episode of the sixth season, "The Forget-Me-Knot." Diana Rigg had declared before shooting started on the fifth-season series that it would be her last. Thus the producers were able to plan a motivation for Emma Peel's termination of her relationship with John Steed. Late in the episode a newspaper headline announces, "Peter Peel Alive: Air ace found in Amazonian Jungle." The episode's end tempered the pathos of Steed and Peel's parting humorously by suggesting that Peter Peel appeared to be remarkably similar to Steed:

Steed in his study, on the phone.

STEED: "Yes, Mother, I've seen the papers. Yes, it looks as though I'll be needing a replacement. As soon as possible." *Smiles as he listens.* "You know my taste. I'll trust your judgment."

He hangs up and picks up a newspaper. His point of view on the head-line: "Peter Peel Alive: Air ace found in Amazonian jungle. Wife Emma waits."

Steed sighs and looks off at the sound of a door.

EMMA *enters:* "Steed?" *Joins him.* "You've seen the newspapers? Trust him to make a dramatic reappearance. Found in a jungle."

STEED, *smiling:* "The Amazonian jungle."

EMMA: "Corny."

STEED: "Ridiculous."

EMMA: "They've flown him back. He'll be picking me up in a few minutes."

STEED: "Here?"

EMMA, *standing close to him, quietly:* "Always keep your bowler on in times of stress. Watch out for diabolical masterminds."

STEED: "I'll remember."

EMMA, *whisper:* "Good-bye, Steed." *Kisses him on the cheek and turns to leave.*

STEED: "Emma." *She turns.* "Thanks." *She smiles and leaves. Hold on Steed, his eyes brimming with tears.*

On the stairs, Emma meets Tara, her replacement.

TARA: "Apartment 3?"

EMMA: "At the top of the stairs." *Tara starts up.*

EMMA *pauses:* "Um. He likes his tea stirred anti-clockwise." *Mimes this with finger. Tara also circles with finger, smiles, and continues up. Emma exits.*

Steed at the window. From his point of view, we see Emma join a man in a bowler hat, who lets her into a convertible and gets into the driver's seat, all without his face becoming visible. Emma waves up toward the window. Steed squints, puzzled, trying to see the man. The car pulls away. Steed smiles, Emma smiles back, and the car pulls away into the distance.

In the 1960s it was quite rare for a series to have a final episode providing closure. Another exception, the TV version of *The Fugitive*, ended in 1967 with a solution to the crime that had been the basis of the series since the premiere in 1963.[19] Such wrap-up episodes for series became more common in the late 1970s, especially with sitcoms like *The Mary Tyler Moore Show* and *The Bob Newhart Show*.[20] On reflection I realize that the makers of *The Avengers* had an important reason for explaining Mrs. Peel's departure. Given that Steed was taking up with a new female partner in the sixth season, it was necessary to show that he had not simply thrown over Mrs. Peel in favor of another woman. Hence her happy departure with her long-lost husband.

In contrast, the film of *The Avengers* ends with the suggestion of a continuing romance between Peel and Steed. The fact that Mrs. Peel is presumed to be a widow since her test-pilot husband disappeared over the Amazon jungle is mentioned at one point. By the end there has been no word of his miraculous return. Given that Mother, Peel, and Steed are sipping champagne together at the end, we are presumably to believe that the Ministry team has survived and can go on fighting future villains. In an earlier scene Peel and Steed had kissed, but that had been interrupted by the villains and the romance had no chance to develop. Here, at the very end, they apparently become a romantic couple and hence perhaps a regular crime-fighting team as well:

London at dawn, the Houses of Parliament and the Thames. On the river, large bubbles rise, and a round submarine contraption pops up. The "Avengers" theme music swells up.

Cut inside the submarine. Steed and Emma smiling at each other.

STEED: "The owl and the pussycat went to sea . . ."

EMMA: ". . . in a beautiful pea-green boat."

STEED, *looking out at the dawn:* "A perfect morning. Bit chilly. I think we deserve some champagne."

Close view of Emma smiling. Cut to an extreme long shot of Tower Bridge with the submarine floating. A second cut on the sound of a cork popping leads to a close shot of Mother pouring champagne.

MOTHER, *lifting a glass:* "A toast! To a job well done."

Steed and Emma stand together with champagne glasses.

EMMA: "To a narrow escape!"

MOTHER, *to Emma:* "Macaroon?" *[a reference to a motif set up early in the film]*

EMMA *shakes her head, glances at Steed, and raises her glass:* "Thank you, Steed."

STEED, *smiling:* "No, thank *you*, Mrs. Peel."

Gazing into each other's eyes, they clink glasses and sip champagne.

Extreme long shot, with zoom out from a small gazebo on the roof of a large building by the Thames.

Indeed, it has become conventional in recent movies to achieve closure in the main story while either introducing a new dangling cause at the very end or hinting that such a cause could occur soon. In both the original *Buffy* film and the final Peel episode of *The Avengers*, major characters exit in the classic way, away from the camera on a vehicle into the distance, presumably not to be seen again.[21] The adaptations end differently, with the characters gathering to discuss the future—explicitly in *Buffy* and merely implying new and continuing relationships in *The Avengers*. Obviously any producer wants to keep the option of making a sequel should the first film become a hit. Presumably in the case of *The Avengers*, the filmmakers hoped the film would be successful enough to allow them to make further films, possibly establishing a comic spy series comparable to the James Bond series. The film's disastrous reception undoubtedly ruled that out, but the ending clearly prepares the way for possible sequels.

The *Buffy* adaptation, on the other hand, has been very successful and provides a model of how modern media interact to generate potentially endless narrative material from a single basic situation. Recently a Saturday-morning children's animated version of *Buffy* has been announced. This time slot has provided extended lives for other movie-originated characters, as in the cartoon series *Beetle Juice* (based on Tim Burton's 1988 feature).[22]

SEQUELS, SERIES, SERIALS, SPIN-OFFS, AND SAGAS

As the example of *Buffy the Vampire Slayer* shows, the issues of adaptation, sequels, and serials are closely related. In a way, these forms would appear to indicate that films and television series are moving closer together in their ways of telling stories. That may well be true. Most likely the expansion of moving-image sequels and serials reflects the need of modern media—print and image— to get as much mileage out of any single narrative property as possible.

Sequels have, if anything, a worse reputation than do adaptations. They usually are seen as an attempt to milk the success of one film by making a second that will probably not live up to the original's quality and success. This is unfortunately often true, but it is far from invariable, and the growing number of sequels will inevitably increase the chances of at least some being good. And film sequels have respectable precedents in the other arts. Shakespeare clearly realized that he was onto a good thing with Sir John Falstaff and brought him back. The text we have of *Don Quixote de la Mancha* includes both an initial novel and its sequel. Cervantes ends the first book with a dangling cause, describing the supposed lack of further documents concerning the Don's adventures: "But the author of this history, although he has made a most thorough and diligent search, has been unable to come upon any account—at least none based on authentic sources—of the deeds performed by Don Quixote on his third sally." The last line of the book suggests that the author and his readers can "hope that we may be given an account of Don Quixote's third sally." And of course part II, published ten years later, begins with an account of the third sally. In more recent centuries, *The Adventure of Huckleberry Finn* was a sequel to *The Adventures of Tom Sawyer*, and *The Lord of the Rings* was a sequel to *The Hobbit*. Thus sequels should not be entirely dismissed as a format, even in film and television.

Within the history of the cinema, sequels occurred fairly early. Mauritz Stiller's charming 1917 Swedish comedy *Thomas Graal's Best Film* was so successful that the following year he made *Thomas Graal's Best Child*. In Hollywood, Universal's lucrative horror wing brought forth such sequels as *Bride of Frankenstein* (1935). Warner Bros. followed its popular family drama *Four Daughters* (1938) with *Daughters Courageous* (1939) and two further sequels.

Nevertheless, the period when sequels became a regular and fairly frequent strategy for Hollywood studios began in the 1970s.

What caused this new trend? One possibility is simply that the film industry had gone through a crisis in the late 1960s and was trying new strategies to regain its audience. Capitalizing on the success of certain titles would be one such strategy. Another reason might be that the old Hollywood production firms were in the process of being bought up by big conglomerates during that decade, and new business practices may have dictated an "efficient" use of narrative material. One early example of a sequel, *The Godfather Part II* (1974), came about because the first film had been unexpectedly successful. *The Godfather* (1972) had been based on only part of Mario Puzo's novel, so the sequel employed scenes that had not been used (primarily involving the young Vito Corleone as played by Robert DeNiro), as well as newly created material tracing Michael's subsequent career.[23] Having the rights to all *The Godfather* saga, in and out of Puzo's novel, facilitated Paramount's production of the second film, as well as another sequel based primarily on material not in the original novel.

A high proportion of the really popular films since the 1970s have been followed by sequels, although sometimes with long intervals between them. Much was made of the fact that *Hannibal* (2001), the sequel to *The Silence of the Lambs* (1991), premiered on the tenth anniversary of the release of the original film. *Titanic* (1997) has yet to spawn a sequel, but one can never tell. Certainly the many jokes made about what shape such a sequel might take suggest that the public recognizes that successful films and sequels often go together.

Ultimately (or perhaps I should say, so far), there have been three *Godfather* movies. This example raises the question of where sequels end and series begin. The issue is not trivial, for it points to the area where film and television have created new possibilities for complicated, if not necessarily complex, narratives. If

Mad Max II (also known as *The Road Warrior* [1981]) follows *Mad Max* (1979), we clearly have a sequel. When *Mad Max Beyond Thunderdome* (1985) appears, is that also a sequel, or part of a series? If we count the third film as a sequel, what would we make of the fourth Mad Max movie constantly rumored to be in the works? Does *that* make the sequels into a series? Yet clearly one can have sequels within series. To take a familiar example from literature, P. G. Wodehouse's Jeeves and Bertie narratives constitute a series, yet within that series certain novels are sequels to certain others. *Stiff Upper Lip, Jeeves,* published in 1963, is explicitly a sequel taking place immediately after the action of *The Code of the Woosters,* from 1938—yet four other Jeeves and Bertie novels had been published in between.[24] We might say that a sequel must have some sort of continuing action from the original (as did *Bride of Frankenstein* and *Daughters Courageous*), but most films and books do not include a setup for a future plot (as in the James Bond series). Certainly the end of *The Code of the Woosters* does not leave any dangling cause, and it was not until about twenty-five years later that Wodehouse needed a plot idea and decided to draw on characters and settings from one of his best books. As this example suggests, there is probably no absolute distinction to be made between sequels and series; there is a fuzzy area in between.

An added complication is the recent popularity of what have been dubbed "prequels." Again, these are not entirely new. To continue with the example of the Jeeves and Bertie series, Wodehouse had written three short stories before he realized that he had a winning combination on his hands, one that could provide the basis for a long-running series. He then wrote "Jeeves Takes Charge," a prequel that explains how Jeeves and Bertie got together. Undoubtedly prequels have become more common recently, however. For example, the Hong Kong film *A Better To-*

morrow III (Tsui Hark, 1989) is in fact a prequel to *A Better Tomorrow* (1986), exploring earlier events in the life of one protagonist, who had died at the end of the first film. Thus even narratives that seem to close off all possibility of continuation can provide the seeds for further storytelling.[25]

To top all this off, series can be sequels to other series, as happened with *Star Trek: The Next Generation*, which premiered in 1987, eighteen years after the end of the original series. Moreover, a feature film, *Star Trek: Generations*, appeared in 1994 and filled in narrative links between those two TV series.

Narratives that span several media—film, television, comic books, novels—are sometimes referred to as "sagas." In some cases the novels are not simply "novelizations" using the same plots as the films or television episodes; instead they create new narratives that devoted fans would consider part of the saga as a whole. (The *Star Trek* and *Star Wars* series provide two obvious instances of such sagas.) There are fanzines and Web sites that demonstrate the ability of at least some fans to keep track of the entire range of narratives belonging to a single saga. Indeed, some fans even write unauthorized additions to the saga, distributed through the Internet.[26] In such a situation, narrative seems so dispersed and disunified as to slip away from the possibility of traditional academic analysis, although there are a few scholars who do specialize in such phenomena.[27]

I suspect that the success of sequels in television and especially in film has influenced other narrative arts in recent years. It used to be the case that the death of an author usually meant that no sequel would be written to his or her works. Perhaps the early Holmes stories created by other authors after Conan Doyle's death were the first indication of a change. Certainly by now the death of an author creates less of an impediment to sequels than it used to. In 1991 controversy erupted when the novel *Scarlett*—a sequel to *Gone with the Wind*—appeared, fifty-five years after the original and needless to say by a different author, Alexandra Ripley. One might think that certain narratives would make a sequel impossible to contemplate. *Moby Dick*, for example, seems to make a follow-up difficult by killing off most of its characters. Yet in 1999 *Ahab's Wife* appeared. The latter recalls a similar phenomenon of narrative retelling that has developed in recent decades: a well-known tale presented from a different character's viewpoint. Tom Stoppard used this technique in his play *Rosencrantz and Guildenstern Are Dead* (1967). Gregory Maguire's 1995 novel *Wicked: The Life and Times of the Wicked Witch of the West* makes the villain of *The Wizard of Oz* into its heroine. Stephen Frears's largely overlooked film *Mary Reilly* (1996) reworks *The Strange Case of Dr. Jekyll and Mr. Hyde* as seen by a maid in Jekyll's household.[28] I don't think that these should necessarily be called sequels, but then I can't think what else to call them. The closest word might be "spin-off," a term most often applied in common parlance to television. Indeed, the willingness of modern authors to rework or extend the writings of their predecessors may stem from the fact that so many narratives in film and especially television are the work of writing teams. The association of a famous title with a single author perhaps no longer seems as sacred as it once did.[29]

What, then, of serial narratives? It is possible that the vogue for sequels, series, and serials in film reflects an influence from television. The four *Lethal Weapon* films (1987, 1989, 1992, and 1998) somewhat resemble a TV buddy-cop series, with fairly closed narrative adventures. These films also, however, incorporate the mild seriality of much series television, with the characters and their situations gradually changing: the Danny Glover character giving up the idea of retiring, the Mel Gibson character marrying, and so on.

In Chapter 2 I argue that seriality marks a crucial difference between television and film. Of course in the past literary works were often serialized,[30] and film serials enjoyed a big vogue in the 1910s and 1920s, sinking to a low-budget format that lasted into the 1950s; radio serials were an even more long-lived format. As television grew in popularity during the 1950s, however, serials in other arts declined, and in the latter half of the twentieth century, it seems safe to say that TV was far and away *the* art form of seriality.[31] Continuing narratives were originally associated primarily with soap operas, but by now they are common in other genres as well.

There have been attempts to revive seriality in the other arts, but these are so rare as to prove the point that this format has gone over to television. Stephen King released his novel *The Green Mile* as a series of small paperback books (1996), but many readers simply bought them as they appeared and waited to read them until they had the whole set; it was also eventually issued as a single volume (1997). King's much-publicized attempt to serialize a novel over the Internet was discontinued in mid-narrative.

The few true film serials that have appeared in recent decades have been quite successful. One was the *Back to the Future* series (1985, 1989, 1990), which used traditional cliffhangers at the end of its first two parts and resolved the story in the third. Far and away the most successful film serial has been the ongoing *Star Wars* series. George Lucas has not only undertaken the production of nine films in serial format but has managed the unusual—perhaps unique—feat of releasing them out of order. Episodes 4, 5, and 6 were followed by 1, and if the series is completed, we should see 2, 3, 7, 8, and 9. Yet Lucas has stretched his project over decades, and the logistics of making such a serial in this day and age could be undertaken only by someone with enormous resources. Certainly the lengthy film production schedules of contemporary Hollywood films make it difficult to use the same cast for a series of features. Indeed, two serials currently in production show how producers are attempting to cope with this problem. The film adaptation of *The Lord of the Rings* is taking the untested approach of shooting all three parts at the same time, thus gambling a large budget of around $300 million on the hope that the first film released will draw large audiences to the two others, released at one-year intervals. The success of *The Matrix* (1999) has led to two further films, also currently being shot simultaneously—the same strategy that Robert Zemeckis had used for the second and third film of the *Back to the Future* serial. I suspect that both these new projects will be hugely successful and perhaps lead to a renewal of the film serial, now with big-budget, "event" movies.[32]

It is apparent, then, that the tendencies toward adaptations of stories among media, toward sequels, and toward seriality are all part of a general stretching and redefinition of narrative itself. In particular, the notion of firm and permanent closure to any given narrative has loosened across media. Series television, with its broad possibilities for spinning out narratives indefinitely, has been a major impetus in these tendencies. They, along with the innovations in interwoven multiple plotlines discussed in the last chapter, seem to me some of the most intriguing areas where an analyst might explore the aesthetic specificity of series television.

THE STRANGE CASES OF

DAVID LYNCH

IS THERE AN ART TELEVISION?

In any comparison of the aesthetic traits of film and television, the name David Lynch will most likely spring to mind. During his career, Lynch has swung between experimental projects and more mainstream work. *Blue Velvet* and *Twin Peaks* marked a period of about five years in which he established his reputation as a director of "weird" tales that drew considerable attention from the public and the press.

The two works contain enough similarities to make comparison relatively easy. Both are mysteries set in small lumbering towns, and their two protagonists share some traits and are played by the same actor, Kyle MacLachlan. He has recalled, "Someone said to me that they thought Dale Cooper was Jeffrey Beaumont grown up."[1] One might easily get that impression, though Cooper's intelligence distinctly outstrips Jeffrey's. The similarities between the two works have given rise to a considerable body of writing, primarily thematic interpretations of them as quintessentially

Lynchian. *Blue Velvet* and *Twin Peaks* are widely assumed to be his best works, and this is a plausible appraisal.

What more can we learn from such a comparison? I have long been fascinated by the issue of how avant-garde works occasionally emerge within a purely commercial context. Shortly after the end of World War I, the German film industry produced *The Cabinet of Dr. Caligari* (1920) and a whole series of Expressionist films. Similarly, Eisenstein's *Potemkin* (1925) and Carl Dreyer's *La Passion de Jeanne d'Arc* (1928) were made by profit-oriented companies in the 1920s. Following World War II, often with the help of government subsidies, an art cinema emerged, initially in Europe and Asia, that has remained as an alternative to mainstream Hollywood-style filmmaking ever since. Here I am using "art" in a much more narrow and conventional sense than in the first chapter, where I referred to fictional television programs as "art," whether good or bad.

We all have a general sense of what "art films" are. They are usually small-scale productions that appeal primarily to an educated audience, often outside their country of origin. They are usually made and exhibited within a set of institutions separate from those of mainstream commercial films. In Britain the lottery now helps support them; in France a tax on cinema tickets funds them. There are special "art cinemas" devoted to them in cities and university towns. An international film-festival circuit has burgeoned in recent decades, meaning that Iranian or Japanese films can be seen in dozens of countries without ever playing in an actual theater. Certain video companies specialize in art films, for example, Artificial Eye and the British Film Institute in the U.K., and New Yorker and Kino International in the U.S.

Art films form a sort of middle ground between mainstream

commercial films and pure experimental cinema—the latter being the kind of personal, often non-narrative films that screen mainly in museums and filmmaking cooperatives. Some art films are daring enough that they approach experimental work—say, some of Jean-Luc Godard's films of the late 1960s and early 1970s or the films of Vertov and Eisenstein in the USSR during the 1920s. At the other end of the art-film spectrum lie films that are subtitled or in other ways "arty" but that nevertheless manage to find a larger audience, something *Life Is Beautiful* (1997) did a few years ago and *Crouching Tiger, Hidden Dragon* (2000) is currently doing.[2] Such films draw in art-cinema lovers, but also a share of the mainstream market as well.

Can the same phenomenon occur in television? Can there be "art TV" that airs on the mainstream networks? Certainly there is no clearcut set of alternative institutions within the television establishment. Government-supported systems like the BBC have a mandate of sorts to create quality television, but that might just mean the sorts of prestigious miniseries exported to fill the schedules of the public broadcasting system in the U.S.—adaptations of Dickens or Austen, for example, which are comparable to the "prestige" literary adaptations of Hollywood's studio era (as with MGM's 1936 *Romeo and Juliet* and its 1940 *Pride and Prejudice*). That is not the sort of television I am referring to as "art television." What I mean is a sort of television comparable to art films.

Given the current widespread application of the term "postmodern" to television, I should specify that what I am calling "art television" is not synonymous with "postmodern television." There are two main ways in which television is argued to be postmodern.

Some claim that a postmodernist quality arises from the overall flow of programming, which juxtaposes disparate items: fiction next to nonfiction, comedy next to drama, commercials next to programs. Thus the format of TV scheduling creates the jumble that has a postmodern effect of reflexivity, irony, and so on. If this is the case, individual programs are not the source of this postmodern effect, and hence they would still be subject to isolation from their place in a schedule and to formal analysis of the type I have been proposing.

A second approach holds that certain individual series are instances of postmodernism, which is then presumably only intermittent across all of TV. In that case, one could sort out which programs are postmodern and which are not. Interestingly, the programs sometimes cited as postmodern—*Late Night with David Letterman, Saturday Night Live*, music videos, commercials—are often not narrative programs.

Nevertheless, if any narrative program could be claimed to be postmodern, it would certainly be *Twin Peaks*, which has influenced other eccentric series like *Northern Exposure* and *The X-Files*. *Twin Peaks* has an imbedded soap opera, *Invitation to Love*, which roughly parallels its own events. For example, when Hank shoots Leo Johnson in the first-season finale, Leo lies bleeding and watches a thug get shot on *Invitation to Love*. Reflexivity and irony are working full throttle here.

If postmodernism is to be found in individual programs, then these programs are presumably also isolable from the scheduling flow and available for analysis. (Indeed, how could one differentiate postmodern from non-postmodern programs without at least cursory analysis?) I have no objection to analysts looking for postmodern television in this way, but my interest here is different. "Art cinema" is a term in wide public usage, and it implies specific and well-established conventions. I wish to examine whether some of those same conventions occasionally appear in commercial television. This would seem to be a more limited issue than whether television as a whole or some television programs in particular are postmodern. "Art television" might well be considered by some a subcategory of postmodern television. That is, postmodern conventions may now be so pervasive as to constitute a new set of popular norms long since assimilated by many viewers, but art television might have ambiguities and other challenging techniques that stretch or break those conventions. At any rate, for now I am dealing with only how we might define "art television," postmodern or not.

Before tackling my main subject, David Lynch's *Blue Velvet* and *Twin Peaks*, I would like to define more specifically what I mean by "art films" and give you a brief, clear-cut example of how that definition could be applied to television. Several traits of art films were laid out by David Bordwell in his 1979 article "The Art Cinema as a Mode of Film Practice." I shall apply his outline of traits not to a film, but to a classic of British television, the 1986 BBC miniseries *The Singing Detective*. If there have been any instances of art television in the Anglophone history of the medium, this one definitely figures high among them.

THE SINGING DETECTIVE AS ART TELEVISION

Bordwell discusses five major traits as typical of the art-cinema mode: a loosening of causality, a greater emphasis on psychological or anecdotal realism, violations of classical clarity of space and time, explicit authorial comment, and ambiguity.[3]

The Singing Detective certainly eschews the linear cause-and-effect chain typical of classical narratives. It moves freely among three basic levels. The "real" situation has the protagonist, Philip Marlow, suffering from a painful skin disease and confined to a hospital. He is also suffering mental problems, as we learn in part from scenes of his imagined reworking of his published potboiler, *The Singing Detective*. On a third level, flashbacks from his childhood, also revised by his imagination, display reasons for his adult problems.[4]

The fantasy elements that run so strongly through the series would seem to preclude realism. Yet *The Singing Detective* also focuses on the painful details of Marlow's skin disease and its treatment, the illnesses and deaths of his fellow patients, and ultimately on his emergence from fantasy into health and a departure from the hospital. Moreover, the narrative appeals to the art cinema's deeper form of realism, character psychology. Few film or television narratives have spent so much time probing the fantasies, delusions, and traumas of a protagonist. Bordwell's discussion of art cinema suggests that the typical hero procedes through an itinerary: a journey, a search, the making of a film. *The Singing Detective* traces Marlow's parallel physical and mental cures; we see the gradual improvement of his skin, just as we see him open up to the hospital psychologist and finally reconcile with his wife.[5] In some ways *The Singing Detective* resembles the classic art film *8½* (1963). In Fellini's film the hero, Guido, is trying to make a film but cannot, and his fantasies—including scenes from his youth—expose and explore his problems.

The Singing Detective constantly violates classical notions of redundantly marked shifts in space and time. It freely cuts among fantasy and reality, past and present. Initially the fantasies appear to be confined to a separate space of film-noir settings in which *The Singing Detective* narrative plays out in Marlow's imagination. Soon, however, his fantasies begin invading the hospital ward as well, with the doctors and nurses suddenly breaking into a song and dance number.

Bordwell emphasizes the importance of the author in the art cinema:

> Not that the author is represented as a biographical individual (although some art films, e.g., Fellini's, Truffaut's, and Pasolini's, solicit confessional readings), but rather the author becomes a formal component, the overriding intelligence organizing the film for our comprehension. Over this hovers a notion that the art-film director has a creative freedom denied to his/her Hollywood counterpart. Within this frame of reference, the author is the textual force "who" communicates (what is the film *saying?*) and "who" expresses (what is the artist's *personal vision?*).[6]

While film is usually held to be a director's medium, television depends more fundamentally on its writers.[7] Commentaries on *The Singing Detective* attribute it to Dennis Potter rather than to its director, Jon Amiel. Interviewers and commentators have tried to read the series autobiographically because the character of Marlow has a skin disease similar to one which afflicted Potter—though Potter denies any resemblance beyond that detail.[8] Certainly the series encourages not only an interpretation of Marlow's character but also an interpretation of Potter's commentary on his protagonist's psychological progress. The series also draws on Potter's most famous authorial touch, the use of lip-synching to recordings of old popular songs.

Finally, one of the most characteristic traits of the art cinema is ambiguity. If the classical cinema values a clear cause/effect chain, then an uncertainty surrounding how the chain fits together or concludes provides an alternative approach to narrative. In *The Singing Detective*, the increasingly convoluted and dense variations among Marlow's memories, his reworking of his pulp novel, and his fantasies become increasingly intertwined and often difficult to distinguish. For example, early in the third episode, we see a flashback to a scene of the young Marlow riding in a train with his mother after she has left his father. The boy sees a scarecrow wave to him:

Close-up of young Marlow seated by the window of a train. He watches as a group of soldiers in the compartment ogle his mother's knees as she sits opposite Marlow, reading a newspaper.

MARLOW, *heavy country accent:* "Ma? Oh, Ma?"

One soldier, chagrined, looks away. Marlow's mother ignores him. Marlow looks out the window, then at the newspaper. His point of view of headline: "War Rushing to an End!"

MARLOW'S *voiceover [boy's voice]:* "That's bloody old 'Itler done for, then. So everythin'll be all right. That's what them do say, y'know. It'll be a luvly day t'morrah. Wat's it? Bluebirds an' that, over the . . . Everybody says, when the war is over, lights and flowers, butter, eggs, the lot. Comics, sweets, everythin'. It'll be all right, all right, all right."

His POV of the newspaper, voiceover continuing: "The war rushin' to an end, exclamation mark. Oh, I do like me a good exclamation mark, mind."

An extreme long shot of the train moving through the countryside, followed by a medium close-up of Marlow seen through the train window. He looks out. An extreme long shot shows his POV through the window. In a field, a scarecrow with arms outstretched appears against the sky. Ominous music begins. In medium close up as before, Marlow rubs fog off the window with his hand. His POV as before reveals the scare-

crow lowering its left arm and raising the right one in a waving ges-
ture, a motion accompanied by an eery sting in the music. In medium
close-up as before, Marlow continues to look out the window with a
frown.

Dissolve to the adult Marlow's hospital ward.

Aside from the status of the scarecrow vision, we are left to wonder whether the line about liking exclamation marks really repre-
sents the young Marlow's thoughts. Though the line is spoken in
the boy's voice and with the heavy accent that the adult Marlow
has lost, it seems an unlikely thing for this naive country boy to
ponder. We have seen a number of fairly clearly demarcated flashbacks to Marlow's childhood, but here for the first time a fantasy
element enters, and we may wonder: Did the young Marlow have
the scarecrow fantasy years ago, or is the adult Marlow embellish-
ing the event in retrospect? (The live scarecrow becomes a motif
relating to Marlow's youthful terrors.)

The Singing Detective rapidly became an acknowledged classic, but it certainly stands apart from most other television programs—except, of course, some of Potter's other series. The BBC,
with its government funding, would be a logical place to find occasional instances of "art television." One might expect that com-
mercial-network American television, however, would be an odd
place to find them. Yet many films have had dual careers as both
popular hits and art-house classics. The films of the great Japanese directors Yasujiro Ozu and Kenji Mizoguchi were mainstream commercial productions when they first appeared; only
later did they become darlings of Western art-house audiences.
Jacques Tati's comedies were successful with the broad public
from the late 1940s on, and one can still occasionally see *Mr.*

Hulot's Holiday (1953) or *Play Time* (1967) showing at a Sunday family matinee in Paris. Yet from the start Tati also garnered a more esoteric critical admiration somewhat comparable to that afforded his contemporary Robert Bresson. Thus we might expect that in commercial television, as well, the occasional art program might find a crossover audience—especially in the sphere of comedy, where experimentation is easier to accept.

ENTERTAINING UNCERTAINTIES

Twin Peaks would be an obvious candidate for the status of art television. To start with, it has manifest similarities to *Blue Velvet*, which I take to be an art film. *Blue Velvet* was in fact produced by mainstream executive Dino De Laurentiis, who agreed to let Lynch make it as a reward for directing the science-fiction epic *Dune*. According to Lynch, De Laurentiis let him have complete control of the film after he agreed to cut the budget and his salary by half. *Blue Velvet* went on to attract something of a crossover popular audience and to make a modest profit. Lynch was nominated for a best-director Oscar, but *Blue Velvet* did not receive any other nominations. He had apparently slid just within the limits of experimentation that Hollywood could tolerate—as long as his films made money.

Some critics hailed *Blue Velvet* as high art. Pauline Kael declared that Lynch's work "goes back to the avant-garde filmmakers of the twenties and thirties, who were often painters—and he himself trained to be one. He takes off from the experimental traditions that Hollywood has usually ignored."[9] To some extent this statement accurately reflects the film. Lynch's use of slow motion, of dream imagery, and of bright, unnaturalistic color recalls techniques of 1920s German Expressionism or French Impressionism. But there was another side of Lynch that audiences could connect with. That was the explicit sex and violence, the "realistic" facing up to the seamy side of life. Any number of aspiring teenage filmmakers seized on these aspects of Lynch.

Other Lynchian traits most obviously included a highly original taste for the grotesque and the bizarre. We should remember that Lynch was, as Kael pointed out, trained as a painter; he has also created in the areas of photography, performance art, songwriting, and comic strips concurrently with his film and television work. Aside from being well aware of traditions like Surrealism, he was used to approaching his work as personal expression.

Lynch based both *Blue Velvet* and *Twin Peaks* on his own background and obsessions. He places the action of each in a seemingly ordinary small town of the sort where he grew up; he then digs below the surface in search of the hidden, sordid activities of its citizens. The juxtaposition of banal good and overblown evil that results contributes an uncertainty of tone that forms the basis for the underlying ambiguity of both works.

One possible source of the fluctuation in tone in both *Blue Velvet* and *Twin Peaks* is Lynch's idiosyncratic notions of the connotations of many scenes. His interpretations, as revealed in interviews, seem contrary to how one would expect most viewers to take these scenes. For example, in *Blue Velvet* there is a scene in which Jeffrey meets with Sandy after he has witnessed Frank's brutal attack on Dorothy. He has been disillusioned by his discovery that such evil exists, and Sandy tries to comfort him:

Jeffrey with Sandy in her car. He sits brooding dejectedly. Sandy watches him with concern as quiet organ music plays.

JEFFREY, *suddenly:*   "Why are there people like Frank? Why is there so much trouble in this world?"

SANDY: "I don't know. *[Pause]* I had a dream. In fact, it was the night I met you. *[Looks up through the windshield, gradually becoming awed and delighted as she explains the dream]* In the dream, there was our world, and the world was dark because there weren't any robins, and the robins represented love, and for the longest time, there was just this darkness, and all of a sudden, *thousands* of robins were set free, and they flew down and brought this blinding light of love, and it seemed like that love would be the only thing that would make any difference. And it did."

Jeffrey listens, tears in his eyes.

SANDY *looks at him, awkwardly:*   "So, I guess it means, there is trouble till the robins come." *Pause.*

JEFFREY: You're a neat girl."

SANDY: "So are you."

He smiles more broadly.

SANDY: "I mean, you're a neat guy."

Pause as they look at each other and their smiles fade.

SANDY: "I—I guess we'd better go."

JEFFREY: "Yeah, I guess so."

Long shot of the car with a church in the background. Sandy starts the car, and they drive away as the organ music swells slightly.

One common reaction to Sandy's speech and to the film's framing scenes of a glossily perfect small-town life has been an assumption that Lynch is mocking such optimism and perfection. Yet he seems to take these elements in a much more straightforward way:

"I like to have contrasts in a film," explained Lynch, "because there are so many horrific things and so many beautiful things in life . . . Right or wrong, the Dennis Hopper character is, to most people, the coolest character in *Blue Velvet*, and yet there's another side to that picture. The scene in which Sandy tells Jeffrey about the robins is real important to me.

"That scene is kind of embarrassing," he admitted. "Sandy is this emotional kind of girl who gets into this euphoric state which is quite beautiful . . . It's a feeling of what can happen when two people are sitting in a car and falling in love when they're all alone and no one else is listening. They say things like this in a safe environment, goofy things. And I think films should be embarrassing in some places."[10]

Lynch's comment suggests that he realizes that many fans will take the sex and violence to be the essence of his film—that is, they will be fascinated by Frank Booth (played by Dennis Hopper). Yet he seems to intend the treatment of the "good" characters to be quite sincere (i.e., non-ironic).

Another interview, this time concerning *Twin Peaks*, reveals a similar disjunction between Lynch's attitude toward a scene and a more typical interpretation. The interviewer asks Lynch about the famous scene in Episode 3 of the first season, when Cooper lectures on Tibet to the staff of the police department, then throws rocks at a bottle to whittle down a list of suspects:

Cooper, setting up a blackboard in the woods. Lucy, Truman, and Hawk are by a donut-laden table.

ANDY, *with pail, to Cooper:*   "Where do you want these rocks?"

COOPER: "Put 'em right down there by the donuts, Deputy."

LUCY, *proferring a pitcher:*   "Anyone for a warm-up?"

All four men extend cups, with various comments: "Mmm! Ah! You bet!"

COOPER: "Thanks, Lucy."

He sips and spits the coffee out as the others watch.

COOPER: "*Damn* good coffee! And *hot!* Would every one please take a seat."

They move rightward and sit on a row of folding chairs, as if in a class-room. Cooper extends a telescopic pointer.

COOPER: "By way of explaining what we're about to do, I am first gonna tell you a little bit about the country . . ."

He flips over the blackboard to reveal a map of China.

COOPER: ". . . Tibet."

He points to it, and the others lean forward simultaneously.

COOPER, *lecturing earnestly:*   "An extremely spiritual country, for centuries the leader of Tibet has been known as the Dalai Lama. In 1950, Communist China invaded Tibet, and while leaving the Dalai Lama nominally in charge, they in fact seized control of the entire country. In 1959, after a Tibetan uprising against the Chinese, the Dalai Lama was forced to flee to India for his life and has been exiled ever since."

COOPER, *shutting the telescopic pointer:*   "Following a dream I had three years ago, I have become deeply moved by the plight of the Tibetan people and filled with a desire to help them. I also awoke from the same dream realizing that I had subconsciously gained knowledge of a deductive technique involving mind-body coordination operating hand-in-hand with the deepest level of intuition. Sheriff, Deputy Hawk, if you will assist me, I will now demonstrate."

The two rise uncertainly. Cooper flips the map over to the blackboard side.

COOPER: "You may recall, on the day of her death Laura Palmer wrote the following entry in her diary: 'Nervous about meeting J.' Today . . . I'm going to concentrate on the Js." *He circles the J on the board.* "Harry, when I give the word, would you please read aloud each of the names I've written on the blackboard."

TRUMAN: "Okey-doke."

COOPER: "Deputy Hawk, stand over here and hold this bucket of rocks up near me where I can get to them. Would you please put on the kitchen mitts? Deputy Andy, move down, stand by the bottle. Lucy, take this piece of chalk—not too near, Andy!"

LUCY: "I'm getting excited."

COOPER, *to her:*   "—and if I should strike the bottle after Sheriff Truman says a particular name, make a check to the right of that name. Sheriff, I almost forgot. When you say the name, also briefly state that person's relationship to Laura Palmer. Ready?"

LUCY: "Ready!"

ANDY, *off:*   "Ready!"

(As Truman identifies each person, a shot of him or her appears briefly.)

TRUMAN: "James Hurley. Secret boyfriend."

COOPER: "James Hurley." *Throws the rock. It misses, and he takes another.*

TRUMAN: "Josie Packard. Was instructed in English by Laura."

COOPER: "Josie Packard." *The rock misses.*

LUCY: "So . . . there's no check next to either of these names?"

COOPER: "That's correct. Please continue."

TRUMAN: "Dr. Lawrence Jacoby. Laura's psychiatrist."

COOPER: "Dr. Lawrence Jacoby." *The rock knocks the bottle off the stump on which it had been sitting.*

LUCY: "You did it! You hit it!"

COOPER: "Lucy, make a note that the bottle was struck but did not break. Very important. Andy, put that bottle back *exactly* where it was." *Andy does so.*

TRUMAN: "Johnny Horne. Laura was his special-education tutor."

COOPER: "Johnny Horne." *Rock strikes far from the bottle.*

TRUMAN: "Shelley Johnson. Waitress at diner, friend."

COOPER: "Shelley Johnson." *Rock hits stone, ricochets, and strikes Andy in the forehead.*

LUCY: "Oh . . ."

COOPER: "Sorry, Andy."

LUCY: "Sweetie."

ANDY, *breathing hard:* "It didn't hurt. It didn't hurt a bit."

TRUMAN: "Where there's no sense, there's no feeling, Andy."

Andy forces a laugh, continues to breath hard. Cooper takes another rock, and Truman pulls him aside.

TRUMAN: "Coop. Tell me, the idea for all this really came from a dream?"

COOPER, *smiling and confident:*   "Yes, it did." They return to their places.

TRUMAN, *uncertainly:*   "Uh, Jack with One Eye."

LUCY: "Maybe it's the letter I. There's no I in Jack."

COOPER: "I think perhaps it means he only had one eye, Lucy."

HAWK: "Sounds like Nadine—Big Ed Hurley's wife."

TRUMAN: "No, no, no, there's a casino up north called 'One-Eyed Jack's' across the border on the Canadian side."

COOPER: "That's it. We're gonna have to go up there and check that place out."

TRUMAN: "Okay."

LUCY: "Agent Cooper, I'm going to erase this because it's a place and not a person. Actually, maybe the person could be in the place, so should I erase it?"

COOPER: "Yes."

LUCY: "Yes, a person could be in a place or yes, I should erase it?"

TRUMAN: "Lucy!"

COOPER, *raising a hand decisively:*   "Erase it, Lucy. Next name, Harry."

TRUMAN: "Leo Johnson, husband of Shelley, drives a truck, connection with Laura . . . unknown."

COOPER: "Leo Johnson." *The rock smashes the bottle.*

LUCY: "Oh!"

Pause as all consider this. Fade on view of broken bottle.

This scene has often been singled out as indicative of the "weird" qualities of *Twin Peaks*. One interviewer clearly took such a stance when he asked Lynch this question about Cooper's character development: "He starts off kind of straight—a little unusual maybe—and it's not until episode three, when he gives a Zen sermon to the Sheriff's Department in the forest, that you start to realize just how wacky he is. Where did that come from?" Lynch's answer is quite unexpected: "I went to this place in Hollywood where I met the Dalai Lama. And I got fired up about the plight of the Tibetan people. And I told [coauthor] Mark [Frost], 'We've got to do something.' And that whole scene developed out of meeting the Dalai Lama! And then it added another layer to Cooper."[11] We might suspect that in these two cases Lynch is pulling the questioner's leg, but in general his replies during interviews are so forthright that it seems more reasonable to take him at his word.[12] Yet few viewers of *Blue Velvet* or *Twin Peaks* would interpret these scenes as a touching moment of young love and a plea for the restoration of Tibet.

I am certainly not advocating that the artist's intentions should dictate our interpretations of a work. My point is that, at least in some cases, Lynch's notion of what he is doing and the viewer's

notion are miles apart. Here is a man who thinks Sandy's speech
about robins is beautiful, but at the same time he wants it to em-
barrass us. He apparently thinks that Cooper's speech in the forest
is a way of calling attention to the plight of Tibet.[13] If an artist has
views this off-kilter, then it is no wonder that we do not know how
we are to react to certain scenes. Thus in Lynch's work authorial
commentary becomes a major source of ambiguity.

In other cases, however, Lynch quite deliberately creates a mixture of tones. This is perhaps most obvious in the second season
of *Twin Peaks*, where Leland Palmer, the bereaved father, apparently goes a bit mad and breaks out into song and dance routines
in the middles of scenes. This is realistically motivated as a symp-
tom of his grief at his daughter's death, but it also arouses anxiety because of its inappropriateness—the "embarrassment" that
Lynch felt the spectator should feel now and then. Another good
example of a deliberate clash of emotional inflection comes in Episode 1 of the second season. Early in the series a mystery is introduced. Big Ed Hurley, owner of the local garage, is married to
Nadine, an eccentric character obsessed with inventing a silent
drape runner. He loves Norma Jennings, owner of the local diner.
Both Ed and Norma are attractive characters who clearly belong
together, while Nadine is one of the series' oddest, most grating
figures. In a scene from the two-hour premiere of the second season, Ed tells the sympathetic Cooper about the history of his relationship with Nadine, now in a coma after a suicide attempt. Listening nearby are Sheriff Harry Truman, also characterized as a
kindly person, and Albert Rosenfeld, a cynical, tactless FBI foren-
sics expert:

Truman, Cooper, and Albert walk along a hospital corridor.

They find Ed Hurley, sitting disconsolately on a chair.

TRUMAN: "Ed?"

ED *stands, to Cooper:* "How *you* doin'? Heard you stopped a couple."

COOPER: "I'm OK. How's Nadine?"

ED: "Well, she's in a coma. They say there's nothin' we can do, she has to want to come back."

COOPER: "How you holdin' out?"

ED: "Well, all I can do is sit here, thinkin' about the things I shoulda said or done."

COOPER: "Ed, don't be too hard on yourself."

ED: "I never believed in fate, Agent Cooper. Always felt, you make your own way, you take care of your own, you pick up after yourself."

ALBERT: "Farmer's Almanac?"

Truman and Cooper glance at Albert, annoyed.

COOPER: "Albert, I would like to speak to Ed."

TRUMAN, *grim:* "Albert, I'll buy you a cuppa coffee."

Albert and Truman go out right. Ed and Cooper turn away from them.

COOPER: "Take a seat, Ed." *They sit.*

ED: "I saw this comin'. I didn't wanna believe it. What's worse is, I'm sittin' here thinkin' that maybe that there's a parta me that didn't wanna stop her. And that's a full load."

Truman pours coffee. Albert sips his, looks with a puzzled grimace at the cup, and glances at Truman.

COOPER: "When did you get married, Ed?"

ED: "Right out of high school. Norma and I had been together about four years, and everybody figured we'd get hitched, that'd be that. I barely knew Nadine to say hello to."

Truman glances at Albert as the latter sets his coffee aside.

(The next portion of the scene alternates between Ed speaking and Cooper's concerned, sympathetic face, with cutaways to Truman and Albert, nearby.)

ED: "That spring, one bad weekend, Norma ran off with Hank. I was so twisted up inside I couldn't see straight. When I opened my eyes, there was Nadine right in front of me. There was somethin' so sweet, so helpless about her. We drove all night. Ended up in some little town in Montana out past Great Falls. And I asked her to marry me, half jokin', half drunk, half crazy. It was light before we found a justice of the peace, and Norma—well, she hadn't even slept with Hank. And the look on her face when she found out. Nadine and I, we went out to my dad's old cabin, up in Eagle Pass . . ."

Cutaway to Truman listening and Albert glancing impatiently at his watch, then rolling his eyes.

ED: ". . . honeymoon. I was hopin' maybe we'd get around to talking about a divorce, annulment, somethin'—but Nadine was so happy. And you know, by golly, I shot out Nadine's eye on that honeymoon."

Cutaway to Albert, blinking in confused surprise.

COOPER: "What do you mean, Ed?"

ED: "Well, the first day we were hunting pheasant."

Cutaway to Truman, still listening, and Albert, glancing at him. Truman glances at Albert.

ED: "Nadine's a crack shot, and we already had a coupla birds, and I felt good shootin', listening to the sound echo and roll down those hills. I fired, and a piece of buckshot skipped off a rock and caught Nadine square in the eye."

COOPER: "Man, that's a tough one."

ED: "She lay across my lap as we drove back to town . . ."

Cutaway to Truman looking at Albert, who is grinning. Seeing Truman's disapproving look, he tries to sober up.

ED: ". . . she never cried, she never blamed me, she never hated me for it."

Cooper glances off at Albert in annoyance. Truman watches as Albert whips out a hankerchief and pretends to wipe his eyes as he breaks down in suppressed laughter.

ED: "Couple months later Norma married Hank, so I don't believe in fate. You make your bed, you sleep in it."

Truman looks disapprovingly at Albert, who has sobered up.

ALBERT: "Sorry."

Cooper puts his hand on Ed's shoulder.

Thus we have scenes like this, where the tone is deliberately mixed, and other scenes where Lynch apparently has created something that seems to him "beautiful"—to use his favorite term—but which may strike a reasonable viewer quite differently.

This wide range of responses elicited by the narrative of *Twin Peaks* was for some viewers quite evocative. One commentator describing the enigmatic character of the Log Lady suggested the layers of affect prompted by the series: "In many ways the Log Lady, incidental character though she is, sums up what *Twin Peaks* was about—absurd but poignant, mundane but surreal, touching on the mystical."[14]

The overall narrative that results from these disparate aesthetic elements is surprisingly unified. Despite some silly moments and tedious subplots in the second season, the series comes across as one of the most daring balancing acts in the history of narrative television. It managed to hold onto its ABC contract as long as it did primarily because much of its audience was able to ignore many of the ambiguities of tone. Apparently they interpreted its grotesque aspects and its excesses as simply humorous. This presumably made the more difficult scenes of *Twin Peaks* less embarrassing to watch, thus dissipating part of Lynch's power as an artist.

A teleplay manual devoted to daytime soap operas refers to *Twin Peaks* as "David Lynch's prime-time spoof of soap opera."[15] In some ways this seems odd, since relatively few of the series' plotlines were clearly supposed to be comic: most notably Nadine's obsession with silent drape-runners and the screwball-comedy triangle of Lucy, Andy, and Dick Tremayne. But when during the first season devoted fans held their *Twin Peaks* parties, they seized on the obviously comic elements of cherry pie, coffee, and doughnuts. The fact that many people, including young women, were eager to wrap themselves in plastic to imitate the victim of sexual torture and murder suggested that they were not taking the narrative very seriously. I suspect that some of the second season's episodes played into this mocking appreciation by fans, but by that point many in this contingent had already abandoned *Twin Peaks*. Those of us who valued the series for its range of tones did not welcome the introduction of easy humor, and fortunately the later episodes downplayed it in favor of the series' gothic and grotesque elements.

LYNCH'S TAKE ON TV SERIALITY

Many critics have noted that *Twin Peaks* contains a mixture of several television genres.[16] The series' fundamental lines of action combine the soap opera with the detective story. In the soap opera, parallel stories spin out over many episodes, branching and crisscrossing. By starting their series with the discovery of Laura Palmer's murdered body, however, Lynch and Frost undoubtedly created an expectation on the part of the public that the revelation of the killer would not be drawn out excessively.

In fact Lynch and Frost had different ideas about when that revelation should come. On the tenth anniversary of the show's first season, *Entertainment Weekly* interviewed participants for a story of how *Twin Peaks* was conceived, put on the air, and cancelled. Lynch and Frost discussed the Laura Palmer mystery:

> *Lynch:* When we wrote *Twin Peaks*, we never intended the murder of Laura Palmer to be solved . . . Maybe in the last episode.
>
> *Frost:* I know David was always enamored of that notion, but I felt we had an obligation to the audience to give them

some resolution. That was a bit of tension between him and me . . . It took us about 17 episodes to reveal it, and by then people were getting a little antsy . . .

Lynch: All I know is, I just felt it—that once that was solved, the murder of Laura Palmer, it was over. It was over.

Frost: We didn't have an event of similar impact to start the second cycle, and that was to the detriment of the show.[17]

At another point in the same interview, Lynch commented: "A continuing story is a beautiful thing to me, and mystery is a beautiful thing to me, so if you have a continuing mystery, it's so beautiful. And you can go deeper and deeper into a story and discover so many things."[18] This almost goofy infatuation with the possibilities of serial television narratives is hardly in line with the practical demands of network programming.

To understand the opposed viewpoints of the series' two creators, it helps to know that Frost's main accomplishment before *Twin Peaks* was a three-year period as a staff writer for *Hill Street Blues*. As you may recall from Chapter 2, NBC had forced the producers and writers of this program to agree to have at least one of the multiple concurrent storylines achieve closure in each episode. Thus Frost was trained in a format that became widely influential and continues as a norm to this day. He was used to the notion of slowly developing some stories that could eventually come into prominence in later episodes while others developed rapidly within one. It makes perfect sense that he would seek to find "an event of similar magnitude" to Laura's death to carry the beginning of the second season.[19]

In contrast, for Lynch such conventions of television were merely a starting point. One interviewer asked him, "How much of the developing story of *Twin Peaks* was worked out in advance? Did you have a pretty good idea of where it was going?" Lynch replied: "Yes. In TV they have names for everything. Like the 'arc' of the story: where it's going, who's going to do what and all that stuff. And it makes sense to have a plan. So we wrote down our arc, but that's a real general thing. Filling in the blanks is what's so much fun. But the arc satisfies the executives."[20] Apparently for Lynch, Laura's death could provide an arc, but the reactions of members of the community could spin out endlessly developing story lines, with more and more secrets revealed as long as the series lasted. In the *Entertainment Weekly* interview he speaks of revealing the solution to Laura Palmer's murder in the "last episode"—but for a successful prime-time network show, that last episode might be years away.

Lynch seems to have gotten his way to a considerable extent in the final shape that *Twin Peaks* took. Not only was the killer of Laura Palmer kept secret for longer than Frost would have wished, but the revelation was not a full resolution of the mystery: Leland indeed has murdered his daughter, but only, as we realize, because he is possessed by an evil being named Bob who has the power to move from one body to another. In effect Bob is a serial killer who apparently cannot be defeated—obviously a strong force against closure! As the second season develops, it becomes clear that Bob is connected with a mysterious set of seemingly extraterrestrial or supernatural forces centered in the Black Lodge, located in Ghostwood Forest. The possibility of stopping the string of murders seems to rest with Cooper's ability to penetrate this mysterious place and perhaps defeat Bob. When he fails to do so, he himself becomes possessed by Bob at the end of the final episode of *Twin Peaks*. Far from stopping the string of murders, Cooper may be doomed to continue them. Thus we are left with what seems to be a classic season-end cliffhanger. Other plotlines of course are also left open.

The effect on the overall shape of the series was that viewers who wanted closure in the mystery got only partial satisfaction. Presumably they, like Frost, expected another strong plotline to take the place of the Laura Palmer murder. Instead the same storylines that had been opened at the start kept developing, often in more grotesque, bizarre, indeed "Lynchian" ways. The mixture of tones, which as we have seen is typical of Lynch's work, became more extreme. Nadine, whose suicide attempt and lost eye began this plot thread on a poignant note, suddenly awoke possessing superhuman strength and believing herself to be a high school student; her comic affair with the teenaged Mike lasted through much of the second season.

In addition, the supernatural elements that had been primarily motivated as dreams, visions, and memories became more central and objective as the second season progressed. Major Briggs, hitherto seen mainly as Bobby's stodgy, estranged father, turns out to have mysterious extraterrestrial contacts (a secret he seems to share with the Log Lady). No doubt the writers' invention flagged a bit midway in the second season, especially in the wanderings of James Hurley in his attempt to find himself. I personally felt that it picked up later. I suspect, however, that many fans were not sorry to see the program go by the time ABC cancelled it well into the second season. Aside from all its other baffling qualities, *Twin Peaks* had manifestly ceased to be interpretable simply as a spoof of soap operas.

Thus one major challenge that *Twin Peaks* posed to conventional TV, alongside its mixture of genres and tones, seems to have been the violation of expectations concerning the nature of seriality. Multiple continuing stories in prime-time dramas have conventionally been established as interweaving plotlines that periodically achieve closure. *Twin Peaks* instead spun each story line out, adding a twist whenever it seemed about to achieve closure. In Chapter 1, I described how the protagonists of art films like *L'Avventura* and *Toto le héros* may not achieve their goals. The plot of *Twin Peaks* is a case of a protagonist pursuing what threatens to be an ever-receding goal. Lynch took advantage of the serial format to explore his personal interests and obsessions— something he had been rewarded for in his films but which eventually lost him the support of both the network and a large segment of *Twin Peaks*'s viewership.[21]

A trait of both *Blue Velvet* and *Twin Peaks* that seems fairly common in art films and by extension in art television as well is that the author parodies common conventions of classical storytelling technique. One of my favorite examples comes when *Blue Velvet* plays on the classic dialogue hook, which you may recall is a line spoken at the end of one scene designed to provide a clear causal transition to the next. In this short segment, Jeffrey has found a severed human ear and has taken it to the police station, where a coroner examines it:

Coroner's laboratory. The Coroner, Jeffrey, and Detective Williams looking at the ear on a table.

CORONER: "The person may very well still be alive somewhere."

JEFFREY: "What can you tell about the person from the ear?"

CORONER: "Well, once the tests are done, quite a lot. Sex, blood type, whether or not the ear came off a dead person."

A close view of the ear from above.

CORONER, *continuing, off:*   "Also, it look like the ear was cut off with scissors."

NEW SCENE: *close view of scissors cutting a yellow plastic tape reading "Police line do not cross."*

Distant view of the field where Jeffrey had found the ear; a team of people searching the ground as Jeffrey watches.

This dialogue hook does not in fact provide a causal link, since the scissors we see in the opening of the new scene are not the ones that cut off the ear. It creates instead a bit of typically Lynchian grotesque humor.

Twin Peaks parodies the conventions of several genres. As one critic points out, "In audacious soap-opera style, Sheryl Lee, who played the dead Laura, was brought back a few episodes down the line as Madeline Ferguson, Laura's near-identical cousin."[22] A number of scenes poke fun at the convention of recapping action. At the end of the final episode of the first season, the main cliffhanger had consisted of Cooper being shot by an unseen assailant. In the second season, he wakes in the hospital and gets a rundown of the other cliffhanger situations he has missed overnight:

Cooper's POV from his hospital bed. Truman, Lucy, and Dr. Hayward look down at him.

TRUMAN: "Did you get a look at the gunman?"

COOPER, *groggily:*   "I saw a masked face, a muzzle flash . . ." *He shakes his head.*

TRUMAN, *sighs:*   "Lucy, you'd better bring Agent Cooper up to date."

LUCY *opens her notebook and reads:* "Leo Johnson was shot, Jacques Renault was strangled, the mill burned, Shelley and Pete got smoke inhalation, Catherine and Josie are missing, Nadine is in a coma from taking sleeping pills."

Sardonic music begins.

COOPER, *incredulously:* "How long have I been out?"

DR. HAYWARD: "It's 7:45 in the morning. We haven't had this much action in one night since the Elks' Club fire of '59."

This scene also points up the absurdly short duration of the story action in *Twin Peaks*, which extends for little more than a month.[23] Another parody of recapping comes in the earlier scene I quoted: the list of suspects Lucy reads out as Cooper throws stones at a bottle.[24] Such play with narrative conventions seems especially likely to be an attribute of art television, since the medium tends to encourage a great dependence on the formulaic.

Before I leave *Twin Peaks*, I would like to offer one more bit of evidence that it achieved a diverse audience, from general spectators to intellectuals: it is surely the only TV show ever to be the subject of articles in both *Artforum* and *Soap Opera Weekly*.[25]

OTHER ART TELEVISION

So far I have given you only two examples of what I am calling "art television": *The Singing Detective* and *Twin Peaks*. I suspect that there are other such programs, rare though they be. Let me offer you two more candidates—one British, one American. Both programs center on families, but their narrative strategies could hardly be more unalike.

I would put *The Royle Family* into the category of art televi-sion.[26] The six episodes of the first season conform to many of Bordwell's characteristics of the art cinema. The series appeals to anecdotal realism, with its subject matter being the everyday do-ings of a working-class family. Indeed, its style vaguely recalls the *cinéma verité* television documentaries that plant cameras in real families' homes. It departs from the conventions of televisual time and space, confining itself to the interior of the Royle house and playing out each 28-minute episode in continuous, real time.[27] About the only convention of classical storytelling to which *The Royle Family* seems to adhere is consistency of character traits—traits that generate what constitutes the action of each episode.

The most distinctive aspect of the series is its lack of continuing causal lines, which in an ordinary series would be the primary source of dramatic conflict. In Episode 1, two dangling causes are introduced: the daughter Denise's wedding is coming up in six weeks, and the mother, Barbara, is about to embark on a part-time job at a bakery. These would seem to be the sorts of events that could trigger conflict. Given that the husband Jim immediately reveals himself to be a nagging tightwad, we might anticipate that at some point he will rebel against paying for the costly wedding. Barbara's employment may cause family problems because she cannot always be at home to cook for the others. Neither of these ever comes to anything. Jim grumbles about the wedding ex-penses but never even hints that he might not pay. Barbara appar-ently not only manages to keep her family fed but delights them by occasionally bringing home free pastries from the bakery. Even the most obvious source of drama, Denise's decision to call off the wedding at the beginning of Episode 4, is defused halfway through the program when she reconciles with Dave and the fam-ily clusters as usual around the television. Consistently the main conflicts are bouts of petty bickering that blow over quickly. Essentially the program focuses on the family routines rather than on important events, and the development is more motivic than it is causal. Here we have an example of art television that takes almost exactly the opposite tack from *Twin Peaks*, where causal chains divide and develop with extraordinary speed.[28]

Finally, I would like to suggest one more example of a program that at least some people would consider contains elements of art television. *The Simpsons* is a clear-cut case of a program that incorporates different levels of appeal.[29] Its barrage of cultural references probably goes unnoticed by many viewers. Indeed, in the official fan guides to the series, the description of each episode comes complete with lists of "The Stuff You May Have Missed" and "Movie Moments."[30] The series' bizarre plot logic and the blatant inconsistency of Homer's character often run counter to classical storytelling, but they are no doubt acceptable to many viewers simply because the program is a comedy.[31] The phenomenon is reminiscent of the era when the Marx Brothers' 1930s movies and the Ritz Brothers' *Hellzapoppin'* (1941) were admired by both popular audiences and the Surrealists.

I would not claim that all *Simpsons* episodes are transgressive, for they fluctuate considerably between fairly conventional narratives and completely absurdist fantasies. In particular the show's writers take advantage of the annual "Treehouse of Horror" Halloween specials to create three short segments that often abandon the basic premises of the series and become downright experimental.[32] One of the most bizarre of these episodes is the second part of "Treehouse of Horror V" (30 October 1994), when Homer is zapped back to the Jurassic age as he tries to repair a toaster. Squashing a mosquito, he returns to the present to discover that his tiny action has altered evolution and created an alien world. The rest of the episode consists of Homer whizzing back and forth between the distant past and the present, each time determined not to change anything; along the way he generates a dizzying set of evolutionary outcomes. This brief narrative is essentially nothing but a set of variations on the importance of cause and effect. Even within the more straightforward episodes, the characters frequently comment on the conventions of television narrative. There are many examples, but I have narrowed them down to two.

In one, the ugly bartender Moe has undergone plastic surgery and become a handsome soap-opera star. When a piece of the set injured his head, however, he awoke in the hospital with his old face again. As the episode ends, Homer apologizes for his part in the accident that destroyed Moe's handsome face. Moe shrugs this off and remarks on the implausibility of this sequence of events to Homer:

Moe's bar; Homer sits with a beer.

MOE, *behind the bar:* "You did me a favor, Homer. And to think I was about to sell the bar to Hooters."

HOMER: "Yeah, you were—d'oh!"

MOE: "Well, I guess that wraps it up. There's one thing I don't get, though. When my face was crushed, why'd it go back to my old face? I mean, shouldn't it have turned into some kind of third face that was different? Huh! Don't make no—"

Abrupt cut to credits with loud Simpsons theme.

The second scene brings us back to the topic of Chapter 1, for it parodies the idea of flow in television scheduling. It will also serve as a salute to the sponsor of the lecture series on which this book is based, the owner of Fox Television.[33] As fans of *The Simpsons* know, there are many, many satirical references to Fox, its producer, in the show. Again the narrative is just concluding, with Marge explaining how she was able to stop a charging rhinoceros by rolling over her sports utility vehicle. (Stone Phillips, to whom Marge refers, is a news-magazine host on NBC):

Bart, Lisa, Marge, and Homer in a quarry. Officer Wiggam and an Australian hunter join them.

LISA: "How'd you know your plan would work, Mom?"

MARGE: "Thanks for asking. Well, I was watching *Dateline*, and Stone Phillips said SUVs always roll over when you turn sharply, and the gas tanks explode at the drop of a hat."

AUSTRALIAN HUNTER: "And she also knew that if a rhino sees a flame, he'll instinctively try to put it out."

MARGE: "Stone Phillips again."

HOMER, *admiringly:* "Is there anything that guy doesn't know?"

AUSTRALIAN HUNTER: "Why, this Stone Phillips sounds like quite a bloke. What television network is he one?"

BART: "Why, NBC of course."

LISA: "NBC has lots of great shows, and their news and sports coverage can't be beat."

CHIEF WIGGAM, *to Homer:* "Do you think there's anything great on NBC right now?"

HOMER: "Oh, I'm *sure* of it."

MARGE, *turning to address us:*   "But there's only one way to find out!"

Credits roll. During these, we hear the following:

HOMER: "I'd like to read the following statement, *[suddenly defiant]*, but I do so under *[sound of a pistol being cocked; Homer continues, frightened]* my own free will. *[rapidly]* It has come to my attention that NBC sucks. I apologize for misleading you and urge you to watch as many Fox shows as possible. So, in summary, NBC bad, Fox good . . . *[quickly and quietly]* CBS great."

Sound of a gun firing and a body falling, then three more shots.[34]

Here the writers think nothing of killing off one of their main characters for a joke—bringing him back to life, of course, for the next episode.

Programs and series that could reasonably be termed "art television" are no doubt rare, but as a critical category the term is perhaps not useless. I have looked here only at examples that have appeared on network television, but the expansion of cable, with its ability to address niche audiences, will undoubtedly provide new instances.

NOTES

INDEX

NOTES

I. ANALYZING TELEVISION

1. John Hartley, "Housing Television: Textual Traditions in TV and Cultural Studies," in Christine Geraghty and David Lusted, eds., *The Television Studies Book* (London: Arnold, 1998), p. 33.

2. Three of the programs I mention in this book are discussed in George W. Brandt, ed., *British Television Drama in the 1980s* (Cambridge: Cambridge University Press, 1993) in the following essays: John Adams, "*Yes, Prime Minister:* 'The Ministerial Broadcast,'" pp. 62–85; Richard Sparks, "*Inspector Morse:* 'The Last Enemy,'" pp. 86–102; and Joost Hunningher, "*The Singing Detective* (Dennis Potter): Who Done It?" pp. 234–257. Although these essays do not analyze narrative structure in any detail or deal with more popular television programs, they are quite interesting and informative. For a discussion of the place of this type of analysis in the history of television studies, see Charlotte Brunsdon, "What Is the 'Television' of Television Studies?" in Geraghty and Lusted, eds., pp. 97–98.

3. One of the few attempts to theorize television narrative was perhaps the victim of this shift. In her "Narrative Theory and Television" (in Robert C. Allen, ed., *Channels of Discourse: Television and Contemporary Criticism*, 2nd ed. [Chapel Hill: University of North Carolina Press, 1987], pp. 42–73), Sarah Ruth Kozloff offered what was basically a structuralist approach to the subject. She drew on Tzvetan Todorov, Roland Barthes, Vladimir Propp, Robert Scholes, and other theorists

who were influential in the field of film studies in the 1970s and 1980s. The moment when this approach might have been applied to television had, however, passed already, as cultural studies had come to dominate the field.

An introductory textbook that teaches the basic stylistic traits of the film medium is Keith Selby and Ron Cowdery, *How to Study Television* (Houndmills, Basingstoke, Hampshire, England: Palgrave, 1995). Selby and Cowdery take a semiotic approach aimed primarily at interpreting coded meanings in television, narrative and non-narrative.

4. Horace Newcomb and Paul M. Hirsch, "Television as a Cultural Forum," in Newcomb, ed., *Television: The Critical View*, 5th ed. (Oxford: Oxford University Press, 1994), p. 504.

5. Raymond Williams, *Television: Technology and Cultural Form* (1974; reprint, Middletown, Conn.: Wesleyan University Press, 1992), pp. 80–81.

6. Stephen Heath and Gillian Skirrow, "An Interview with Raymond Williams," in Tania Modeleski, ed., *Studies in Entertainment: Critical Approaches to Mass Media* (Bloomington: Indiana University Press, 1986), p. 15.

7. Lynn Spigel, "Introduction," in Williams, *Television*, pp. ix–x.

8. Brunsdon, "What Is the 'Television' of Television Studies?" p. 106.

9. Nick Browne, "The Political Economy of the Television (Super) Text," *Quarterly Review of Film Studies* 9, no. 3 (1984): 177.

10. See, for example, Jostein Gripsrud, "Television, Broadcasting, Flow: Key Metaphors in TV Theory," in Geraghty and Lusted, eds., pp. 28–29.

11. Williams, *Television*, p. 87.

12. Ibid., p. 85.

13. Newcomb and Hirsch, "Television as a Cultural Forum," p. 510.

14. Recent technology like the TiVo system further allows the viewer to reprogram television schedules to suit his or her convenience, and the future of technology can only lead further in this direction. For a summary of technologies currently in development, including PVR (personal video recorder) and S-VOD (subscription video-on-demand), see "Power in Your Hand: A Survey of Television," *Economist* (13 April 2002): 6–8.

Easy-to-use digital technology seems likely to decrease spectators' tendencies to turn on the TV and watch a series of programs. While 90%

of American households have VCRs, they spend only 4% of their TV-viewing time watching programs they record themselves; with the TiVo system, the proportion rises to 70%. (The difference is due in part to Americans' notorious inability to program a VCR's timer.) See "Power in Your Hand," p. 10. Digital technologies for delivering video-on-demand will make the individual program more prominent than ever, as viewers order whole seasons of their favorite series.

15. John Fiske, *Television Culture* (New York: Methuen, 1987), pp. 103-104.

To be fair to Williams, he did discuss channel changing, though he seemingly still considered the viewer a passive consumer of flow: "But the flow is always accessible, in several alternative sequences, at the flick of a switch" (Williams, *Television*, p. 88). He based his claims about flow partly on the idea that people "watch television" rather than watching individual programs (p. 88). It seems more likely, however, that they do both. That is, many people undoubtedly turn on the set to view a stretch of television programming without planning what they will watch. Yet the next day they are more likely to ask their friends, "Did you see *Ally McBeal* last night?" than, "Did you watch TV last night?"

16. For a thoughtful discussion sympathetic to Williams' overall work on television, see Stuart Laing, "Raymond Williams and the Cultural Analysis of Television," *Media, Culture & Society* 13 (1991): 153-169. Laing considers flow to be the main weakness in Williams's approach. Pointing to the many ways in which other scholars have applied the terms, Laing considers that "the problem with 'flow' is that it is a concept which was asked to do too much—to cover too many diverse aspects of the contemporary situation as well as to be the defining characteristic of the medium" (p. 167). For a similar conclusion, see John Ellis, *Visible Fictions: Cinema Television Video* (London: Routledge & Kegan Paul, 1982), pp. 117-118. Ellis proposes instead that television consists of very short (approximately five-minute) segments. This idea is doubtless useful for some purposes but not for my project here, since it does not separate programs from commercials.

Lynn Spigel presents a useful account of flow and its influence on television studies in her "Introduction" to Williams, *Television*, especially pp. xxv-xxvi.

17. Todd Gitlin, *Inside Prime Time*, rev. ed. (Berkeley: University of California Press, 1994), p. 60.

18. A vivid example of programmers' thinking was provided in April of 2001, when the UPN network outbid rival WB for the rights to the latter's successful and long-running *Buffy the Vampire Slayer.* The high price UPN paid per episode guaranteed that the series would lose money, but the actual goal, as reported by *Variety,* was flow: "But [UPN CEO Dean] Valentine is counting on a 'halo effect' from the show. UPN execs believe *Buffy* will add eyeballs to the netlet's entire lineup and subsequently raise the network's CPM [cost per thousand] levels across the board. 'It's a quality show that spreads its golden wings over our entire schedule,' Valentine says. There's plenty of precedent behind that philosophy. NBC, after all, negotiated an astronomical $13 mil per episode to keep *ER* during that show's first renewal, while ABC, CBS and Fox bid record amounts when NFL rights last expired three years ago, arguing that the sport drives young men to the rest of their lineups." Whether one calls it "flow" or a "halo effect," the phenomenon undoubtedly exists. See Michael Schneider, "UPN Bites into *Buffy,*" *Variety* (30 April–6 May 2001): 76.

19. Indeed, in reporting the UPN purchase of *Buffy the Vampire Slayer* as an intended generator of flow, *Variety* continued the passage quoted in the previous endnote: "The halo effect hasn't materialized that frequently in prime time TV, however. The WB hasn't been able to create hits behind *7th Heaven;* NBC's *Friends* didn't make any new ones at 8:30 P.M.; it took years for Fox to capitalize on its football aud; and UPN has yet to steer *WWF Smackdown*'s young fans to other nights of the week." This article demonstrates perfectly how the concept of flow, though not necessarily by that name, is used within the industry itself to analyze the dynamics of whole evenings' or weeks' worth of programming. See Schneider, "UPN Bites into *Buffy,*" p. 76.

At the same time, the creation of giant multimedia conglomerates through mergers and the resulting synergy among the components of those conglomerates have created a new vision of flow. Here loyalty to a channel or set of channels owned by a single huge firm is encouraged by promoting the same series to different age groups. As *Newsweek* noted, "Dub it 'cradle to grave' TV. Media giants are racing to ever more tightly link their cable and broadcast networks to share TV shows, big advertisers and, most important, viewers from across age lines, kids to grandparents . . . It's just the kind of potentially profitable backscratching that advertisers love by linking their fragmented cable and broadcast viewership.

For Big Media, today's holy grail is 'multiplatform' advertising—bundling together in a single purchase ads that can run on cable and broadcast TV, on the Internet and in magazines." See Johnnie L. Roberts, "Cradle to Grave TV," *Newsweek* (19 March 2001): 40.

20. Mike Budd, Steve Craig, and Clay Steinman, "'Fantasy Island': Marketplace of Desire," in Michael Gurevitch and Mark R. Levy, eds., *Mass Communication Review Yearbook* 5 (1985): 297. Aside from the broad, universally applicable narrative patterns employed, there are other problems with this essay. The authors must resort to assuming spectators are affected by such juxtapositions of commercial and narrative without noticing it ("less obviously," as they put it), though it seems unlikely that this claim could be tested effectively. The overall impact on spectators posited is that they "are not only watching 'stories' but also are unconsciously and unevenly working through myths that reinforce dominant cultural values, with all their contradictions" (p. 292). Thus the authors build in an answer to all criticisms of their findings: anything that does not fit the conclusions simply reflects a "contradiction" in the "dominant cultural values." This reminds me of the older but similar tactic of humanistic discourse: whatever does not support an interpretation of a text must be irony.

Budd, Craig, and Steinman do allow that their supposed thematic juxtapositions of commercial and program segments are done "perhaps unintentionally" (p. 294). In a footnote, they suggest that actual production practice follows two guidelines in commercial placement: "Do not place ads for competitors next to one another, and protect advertisers against inadvertent connections with program material (an airline with a show involving a plane crash, for example)" (p. 298n2). Both strictures would militate against meaningful juxtapositions among individual segments of programming.

Indeed, unintentional and unfortunate juxtapositions between ads and programs are sometimes noted sarcastically in the press, hardly a reaction desirable to the networks. *Entertainment Weekly*, for example, ran a brief story on the placement of an ad for the appetite suppressant Meridia amid scenes of *Life with Judy Garland: Me and My Shadows* where Garland struggles with her addiction to diet pills. The magazine even went to the lengths of investigating the company's reaction: "Linder Mayer, spokeswoman for Meridia manufacturer Knoll Pharmaceutical Co., is ruby-faced about the juxtaposition. 'This was a surprise to us,' Mayer says. 'It's unfortunate, because we do take our medicines very seriously and we would not have selected that spot.' May they also be spared the broadcast premiere of *Requiem for a Dream*" (Caroline Kepnes, "Judy Poppins," *Entertainment Weekly* [9 March 2001]: 16). Given such occurrences, it is difficult to picture network programmers weaving their numerous commercials into carefully considered time slots, intending secretly to construct great webs of ideological messages aimed at supporting the dominant ideology (which, for most people who watch a lot of television, probably does not need much support).

Finally, given that commercials by their nature often suggest that their products are fulfillments of fantasies, it is hardly surprising that Budd and colleagues could find them echoing the story of a program based on a premise of fantasy fulfillment. This *Fantasy Island* example was clearly chosen because it does seem to fit the "flow" premise. Even so, its dramatic content meshes with that of the commercials only loosely. I suspect that the example is exceptional and that it would be difficult to find other programs with any noticeable, demonstrably intentional meshing of dramatic content with their accompanying commercials. For instance, the episode of *E.R.* that first ran on 16 April 1998 depicts the hectic, complex, difficult attempts of doctors to cure illnesses and save lives. (One fatality in an operation and one incurable cancer case are among the plotlines.) The third commercial in the ad break roughly sixteen minutes into the program, however, depicts women who are happy, healthy-looking, and able to juggle job and children successfully because they take Advil. This effortless route to health (none of the women are shown actually suffering from pain) would seem to contradict the implications of the program's plot, or, from the sponsor's point of view, the plot contradicts the commercial. No doubt this commercial would jibe better with an episode of *Fantasy Island*, but in a schedule of diverse programming, a simple lack of relations among ads and program plots is probably far more normal. (None of the other five ads and promos run during this same break relates to *E.R.* in any discernible way.)

21. Dale Kunkel, "Children and Television Advertising," in Dorothy and Jerome Singer, eds., *Handbook of Children and the Media* (Thousand Oaks, Calif.: Sage, 2001), pp. 378–380. My thanks to Professor Emeritus Joanne Cantor of the Dept. of Communication Arts, University of Wisconsin–Madison, for this reference.

22. Alan Baddeley, *Your Memory: A User's Guide* (Middlesex, England: Penguin, 1983), pp. 57–60.

23. Rebecca Rupp, *How We Remember and Why We Forget* (New York: Three Rivers Press, 1998), pp. 298–300; Donald A. Norman, *Memory and Attention: An Introduction to Human Information Processing*, 2nd ed. (New York: John Wiley & Sons, 1976), pp. 148–152.

24. Kristin Thompson, *Storytelling in the New Hollywood: Understanding Classical Narrative Technique* (Cambridge, Mass.: Harvard University Press, 1999), p. 12. A more detailed account of the techniques discussed here can be found in the section "Basic Techniques of Progression, Clarity, and Unity," pp. 10–21.

25. Multiple plots are more likely to occur in hour-long programs, but some sitcoms, like *Friends* and *Sex and the City*, often use a C plot for half-hour episodes.

2. THEORY AND PRACTICE IN SCREENWRITING

1. Evan S. Smith, *Writing Television Sitcoms* (New York: Berkley, 1999), p. 93.

2. Jean Rouverol, *Writing for Daytime Drama* (Boston: Focal Press, 1992), p. 38. The "[italics mine]" is Rouverol's editorial insertion. The linkage of Aristotle with script guidelines has recently been taken to its logical conclusion by Michael Tierno in *Aristotle's Poetics for Screenwriters: Storytelling Secrets from the Greatest Mind in Western Civilization* (New York: Hyperion, 2002).

3. Richard Sparks, *"Inspector Morse,"* in George W. Brandt, ed., *British Television Drama in the 1980s* (Cambridge: Cambridge University Press, 1993), p. 90.

4. Richard Levinson and William Link, *Off Camera* (New York: New American Library, 1986), p. 111.

5. Madeline Dimaggio, *How to Write for Television* (New York: Simon & Schuster, 1990), pp. 44–45. Dimaggio is clearly not under the illusion that commercials "flow" into the program for the viewers.

6. Syd Field, *Screenplay: The Foundations of Screenwriting* (New York: Delta, 1979), pp. 8–9.

7. Kristin Thompson, *Storytelling in the New Hollywood: Understanding Classical Narrative Technique* (Cambridge, Mass.: Harvard University Press, 1999), pp. 21–44.

8. Tom Stempel, *Storytellers to the Nation: A History of American Television Writing* (New York: Continuum, 1992), p. 229.

9. Rouverol, *Writing for Daytime Drama*, p. 36.

10. Smith, *Writing Television Sitcoms*, p. 91.

11. Ibid., p. 94.

12. Charles McGrath, "The Triumph of the Prime-Time Novel," *New York Times Magazine* (22 October 1995): 52. McGraph argues convincingly that post–*Hill Street Blues* dramas have incorporated a Dickensian complexity that also achieves something of the realism of the Victorian novel. This occurs partly because such dramas are often set in social and work situations rather than in domestic ones. He also, however, seems to feel he must further justify these programs as "issue-oriented" (p. 55) and even "informative"; he suggests of *ER* that the viewer can "learn a lot about medicine" (p. 56). Given the *Times*'s educated readership, many of whom probably at least profess to look down on TV, perhaps McGrath felt compelled to justify dramas as not only complex constructs but also serious and uplifting art.

13. Certainly there are some multiple-plotline dramas that fail to keep all strands of their narratives clear. Recently *Entertainment Weekly* made the remarkable suggestion that the networks use Saturday evenings—traditionally the night with the lowest viewership—to repeat popular programs, especially ones that have overly complicated plots. In some cases viewers who had missed the original broadcast would tune in. Citing ABC's "knotty spy story" *Alias*, however, the columnist added: "I even suspect, given the knottiness of it all, some fans would start watching both Saturday and Sunday episodes, to double their pleasure and make sure they're clear on the plot." See K. T., "10 Ways to Fix TV: Saturday Night's Alright for Repeats," *Entertainment Weekly* (24 May 2002). This would be a new way to provide redundancy when the program itself does not include enough.

14. Michael Schneider, "TV Takes a Deja View," *Variety* (20–26 May 2002): 1.

15. A relatively early example was the title character's marriage in the 1954 season of *Mr. Peepers*. See Stempel, *Storytellers*, p. 43.

Series are often shown in "stripped syndication," meaning that they are aired daily in the same time slot. Self-contained episodes are ideal for this format, allowing stations to ignore the original order of the series.

16. This use of the term "story arc" should not be confused with the same term as it applied to film narratives; there the arc usually occurs within a single film.

17. Although parts of *The Royle Family* are played for laughs, the overall tone of the program—especially at the ends of episodes—is more poignant than comic. Nevertheless, stores selling videotapes and DVDs of the series inevitably place them in the comedy section. More recently, the last few episodes of the third (and apparently last) series made *The Royle Family* more broadly comic.

18. In recent years, original programming on pay-cable stations has introduced a similar phenomenon in the U.S. HBO's *The Sopranos* and *Sex in the City* have smaller numbers of episodes per season, allowing numerous advantages: "While they admit they'd love to have *The Sopranos*, the networks argue that this isn't really a fair fight. HBO, with only a handful of original programs and seasons that can run as few as eight episodes, has the time and money to nurture its shows. The channel spent $2 million per episode on *The Sopranos* and more than $10 million just to promote this season's premiere. The networks can't match that. They produce 22 hours of weekly programming and seasons with 22 episodes." See Marc Peyser, "Why the Sopranos Sing," *Newsweek* (2 April 2001): 54. The producer of *The Sopranos*, David Chase, has said that he intended from the start that the show would last only four seasons; he planned both the third and fourth series after the end of the second. See Marc Peyser, "HBO's Godfather," *Newsweek* (5 March 2001): 54–55. (Chase bowed to the inevitable and extended the series beyond the fourth season.)

Seasons with small numbers of episodes also have the advantage of fitting neatly into a small boxed set of VHS tapes or DVDs. Short series are, however, discouraged by the fact that studios depend on syndication for profits, and it takes 80 to 100 episodes before a show surpasses its break-even point. Longer seasons make this backlog easier to accumulate. See Lynette Rice, "10 Ways to Fix TV: Less Is More: Short but Better Seasons," *Entertainment Weekly* (24 May 2002): 36.

19. Quoted in John Adams, *"Yes, Prime Minister,"* in Brandt, ed., *British Television Drama*, p. 72. See also Adams's comments on "references across episodes," p. 70.

20. Jason Brett, "Development Hell: The Process of Creating TV in the US," in Julian Friedmann and Pere Roca, eds., *Writing Long-Running Television Series* (Madrid: Media Business School, 1994), pp. 32–33. Brett was a writer/producer for TriStar Television when he gave the 1993 lecture quoted here.

21. P. G. Wodehouse, *Much Obliged, Jeeves* (London: Barrie & Jenkins, 1971), pp. 6–7.

22. Smith, *Writing Television Sitcoms*, p. 100.

23. Rouverol, *Writing for Daytime Drama*, p. 96.

24. Unfortunately the British videotapes of commercial programs I have watched carefully edit out any indication of where the breaks were.

25. This is the last episode of the twelve, which originally appeared as two series of six episodes each. See Garry Berman, *Best of the Britcoms* (Dallas: Taylor, 1999), pp. 14–17; Morris Bright and Robert Ross, *Fawlty Towers: Fully Booked* (London: BBC, 2001).

26. With the expanding practice of releasing entire seasons of popular programs on DVD, the analyst's task should become much easier.

3. THE DISPERSAL OF NARRATIVE

1. André Bazin, "Theater and Cinema" and "*Le Journal d'un curé de campagne* and the Stylistics of Robert Bresson," in *What Is Cinema?* trans. Hugh Gray (Berkeley: University of California Press, 1967), pp. 76–143. The first essay also deals with *Les Parents terribles*, Jean Cocteau's 1948 adaptation of his own play; the second essay deals with Robert Bresson's 1951 film of Georges Bernanos's novel.

2. See my chapter on *The Silence of the Lambs* (1991) in *Storytelling in the New Hollywood: Understanding Classical Narrative Technique* (Cambridge, Mass.: Harvard University Press, 1999), pp. 103–130.

3. I am referring here to theoretical knowledge of cinema; adaptation studies might well be useful to someone trying to learn the craft of screenwriting.

4. Raymond Williams, *Television: Technology and Cultural Form* (1974; reprint, Middletown, Conn.: Wesleyan University Press, 1992), p. 53.

5. Interestingly, many early films depicted the naive reactions of country bumpkins to films (as well as occasionally to plays). Edison's 1902 *Uncle Josh at the Moving Picture Show* (directed by Edwin S. Porter) showed a rube assuming the action on the screen to be actually occurring on the stage. Keystone shorts of the 1910s often exploited the small-town movie audience for humor. This subject matter became less prominent after World War I, when it could be assumed that movies were more widely and frequently seen.

6. In September 2001, UPN premiered *Enterprise*, yet another "Star

Trek" series. *Variety*'s reviewer commented: "By making 'Enterprise' a prequel to the four 'Star Trek' series as well as a follow-up to events introduced in the feature film 'First Contact,' the show not only gives its devoted fans what they love most—continuity monitoring—but rejuvenates a somewhat tired notion." See Laura Fries, "'Enterprise,'" *Variety* (1–7 October 2001): 47. The film Fries refers to is *Star Wars: First Contact* (1996).

7. On Pathé's "scenario crisis," see my "Early Alternatives to the Hollywood Mode of Production: Implications for Europe's Avant-gardes," *Film History* 5, no. 4 (December 1993): 388–389.

8. Today film libraries are so valuable that they are a major factor in studios' planning for a year's worth of production, as *Variety* points out: "A crucial factor of Hollywood math has bedeviled studios for decades: how many releases wind up on the slate. What is the ideal number at which a company maximizes its revenue potential yet also embellishes the value of its library?" (Dade Hayes, "Pics: Any Number Can Play: Studios Shift Gears in Plotting Release Skeds," *Variety* [11–17 June 2001]: 1.)

9. The process of expansion goes on: Warner Bros. became part of Time-Warner, which later became part of AOL (America Online). In 2001, French conglomerate Vivendi (which originated in the nineteenth century as a processor of water and sewage) acquired Universal.

For a chart of the six main media conglomerates that control the major American production firms (current to May of 2002), see Kristin Thompson and David Bordwell, *Film History: An Introduction*, 2nd ed. (New York: McGraw-Hill, 2003), p. 682.

10. The same is true of sequels, prequels, and remakes within the same medium; if a company owns a film, the rights to use it to generate further narratives come along automatically. In 1999, *Variety* surveyed the sources of the fifty top-grossing films of 1998. Its writers concluded, "Only 20% of the top 50 pics were sequels, remakes, or TV spinoffs. However, given the town's growing interest in film libraries, that figure is sure to increase in coming years." See Benedict Carver and Chris Petrikin, "H'wood's Pitches Reap Riches," *Variety* (30 August–5 September 1999): 1.

11. In recent years, an unlikely additional avenue for the exploitation of a single narrative has arisen in the form of Broadway plays (usually musicals) adapted from successful films. Early instances were *42nd Street* and *La Cage aux folles*, and such current hits as Julie Taymor's staging of

Disney's *The Lion King*, Mel Brooks's musicalized version of *The Pro-ducers*, and John Waters's *Hairspray* on Broadway herald many more proj-ects of this sort. Future projects may include *The Pink Panther* and *Bat-man*. See "Great Adaptations," *Entertainment Weekly* (28 May 2001): 28. Relatively few such projects will succeed, of course, but exploiting highly popular stories from other media has become one way of hedging one's bets in the era of huge production costs for live theater. Since touring companies are often the main source of revenues for a play originating on Broadway, a title and story familiar throughout the country is advanta-geous.

On the increasing trend toward turning nonmusical films into plays—typified by *The Graduate*—see Robert Hofler, "Talking Pictures," *Variety* (22–28 April 2002): 39.

12. The difficulty of creating enough series to fill the air time of doz-ens of channels and the high cost of production per episode have led to a recent practice whereby TV production companies sell broadcast rights to a major network, which premieres each episode, and to a smaller cable service, which reruns that episode, sometimes within days of its initial network showing. As of the summer of 2001, for example, *Law & Order: Special Victims Unit* (produced by Studios USA) was running on NBC on Friday nights and again on USA on Sunday night; *Once and Again* (Touchstone TV) played on both ABC and Lifetime. In effect, the pro-duction companies have started to syndicate their series immediately. See John Dempsey, "Shared Runs: Cachet over Cash," *Variety* (11–17 June 2001): 11.

13. This list is modified from part of the more complete Appendix B, "Prime Times Series Based on Movies," in the invaluable reference book *The Complete Directory to Prime Time Network and Cable Shows 1946–Pres-ent* by Tim Brookes and Earle Marsh (New York: Ballantine, 1999), pp. 1269–1274.

14. ABC has recently announced a new series based on *Legally Blonde* (2001). See Johnnie L. Roberts, "Prime-Time Pressure," *Newsweek* (20 May 2002): 46.

15. Similarly, there is a rise in the number of adaptations of older tele-vision series into feature films, which to some extent has paralleled the recycling of these same series through syndication on specialized cable stations in the U.S., primarily Nick at Nite and TV Land. Such cable re-

runs recall to baby boomers their favorite childhood series but also create a new audience among younger people to whom *Charlie's Angels* and *The Addams Family* would otherwise mean little.

16. I have based this list on one in *VideoHound's Golden Movie Retriever* edited by Jim Craddock (Detroit: Visible Ink, 2001), p. 1255, with considerable assistance also from Leonard Maltin, ed., *Leonard Maltin's 2001 Movie & Video Guide* (New York: Signet, 2000). It does not include films based on single programs (e.g., *Joe's Apartment*), television plays (e.g., *Days of Wine and Roses*), or talk shows (e.g., *Ringmaster*). The earliest television-to-film adaptation, *Queen for a Day* (1951), had the peculiar distinction of being a fictional film based on a quiz show involving nonfiction stories told by real people; I have not included it here.

The status of some of the list's films as adaptations from television is admittedly somewhat shaky, as the TV shows themselves were in turn derived from other media (e.g., *Batman* from comic books). The question of what story derives from which version cannot always be answered in this era of multiple exploitations of a single story situation.

17. As of October 2002, *Mission: Impossible 2* was number 18 worldwide and 34 domestically, with a total international gross of $545,300,000. The other films' international grosses are as follows: *Batman*, $413,100,000; *The Fugitive*, $368,700,000; *The Flintstones*, $358,900.000; *Charlie's Angels*, $258,500,000; *Bean*, $232,000,000; *Wild, Wild West*, $217,700,000. (Rankings and grosses are taken from the Internet Movie Data Base, *http://us.imdb.com/Charts/worldtopmovies* and */usatopmovies.*)

18. The primary problem with the film lies with the two main characters. Far from possessing the debonair insouciance of Patrick Macnee's Steed, Ralph Fiennes makes the character seem shy and plagued by inner demons. Uma Thurman's Peel is a bit better, but the "feminist" motif of her defeating Steed at fencing and other competitions destroys the original series' careful balance between the two.

19. The final episode of *The Fugitive*, aired 29 August 1967, remained the highest-rated program until the cliffhanger "Who Shot J. R.?" episode of *Dallas* in 1980. See Allison Hope Weiner, "Silence of the Lam," *Entertainment Weekly* (12 Jan 2001): 20.

"The Forget-Me-Knot" episode of *The Avengers* was not broadcast in the U.K. until 19 January 1969, since it was designed to be the first program of the sixth season. It was shot, however, in January of 1968 and thus might well have been influenced by the ending of *The Fugitive*. Another program that ended with closure in this period was *The Prisoner*, the seventeenth and final episode of which aired on 11 September 1969.

20. The final program of *The Mary Tyler Moore Show* ran on 3 September 1977. *The Bob Newhart Show* wrapped up its characters' situations in a final episode in August of 1978. Most famously, *M*A*S*H* came to an end in a lengthy program on February 28, 1983, drawing the largest audience of any television show to that date.

For dates of American television programs, see Brooks and Marsh, *The Complete Directory to Prime Time Network and Cable TV Shows 1946–Present*; for production information on *The Avengers*, see Dave Rogers, *The Complete Avengers* (New York: St. Martin's, 1989), p. 207.

21. This "ride into the sunset" shot has long been a cinematic cliché conveying closure. (Indeed, it was parodied at the end of each *Avengers* episode, as Peel and Steed departed in some eccentric vehicle.) Yet more recent films use similar shots without implying closure, since they first set up the ideas that the departure is temporary and that the action will resume in a sequel or future installment in the series. In *The Silence of the Lambs*, Hannibal Lecter walks away from the camera and disappears in the distance among the crowd, but the previous phone call to Clarice Starling strongly implies that she will someday try to capture him. Similarly, in *Back to the Future*, Doc departs with Marty and Jennifer in the time machine, which roars away from the camera in the final shot—far above the street's surface. But Doc has first told the pair that he needs their help with a problem in the future, leaving a cliffhanger in a story that developed into a short serial of three episodes. Thus the old image of closure can become a drive toward a new story situation.

22. Even more recently, the struggling UPN network outbid the struggling WB network for the rights to *Buffy*. WB had been paying $1 million per episode, even though the production costs were more than twice that. (As with most modern television programs, the profits would come from later syndication as reruns.) UPN was willing to pay around $2.3 million, even though it could not hope to make a profit at that price. In the strange world of television economics, however, the acquisition was still advantageous, quite apart from its effect on "flow." As *Variety* noted: "Number crunchers note that UPN, while expected to lose money with *Buffy*, will still lose less than had the network put another, new, un-

tested drama in the time period." Michael Schneider, "UPN Bites into *Buffy*," *Variety* (30 April–6 May 2001): 21.

In the days when the three major networks dominated prime time, the cancellation of a series meant its end. With the burgeoning of both free cable and pay services, series have the potential to move from channel to channel. UPN and WB fought over *Buffy* because of its prestige and popularity. Other shows with smaller audiences, however, also can move. What seems like dismal ratings to a major network may look great to a "netlet," as *Variety* calls them. Thus one more institutional encouragement for the perpetuation of narratives expanded during the 1990s.

23. Gerald Gardner and Harriet Modell Gardner, *The Godfather Movies: A Pictorial History* (New York: Wings Books, 1993), p. 132.

24. This does not count *Ring for Jeeves*, the 1953 novel featuring Jeeves but not Bertie.

25. After the 2002 success of *The Scorpion King*, *Newsweek* said of the planned sequel, *Scorpion King II*, "you may need a spreadsheet to follow the chain: it'd be a sequel to the prequel of a sequel of a remake." See John Horn, "Franchi$e Fever!" *Newsweek* (22 April 2002): 59.

26. The increasing trend toward turning movies into videogames creates a new venue for interactive narratives that are somewhat comparable to sequels. Jim Wilson, CEO of Universal Interactive (a division of Vivendi Universal), describes how such games are created using characters and settings from the film but new dramatic situations: "'I don't want to do "See the movie, play the game," because we know how the movie ends,' Wilson says. He points to *The Thing* as an example of how the approach works. The survival-horror game, which is winning buzz in the enthusiast press, starts after the movie ends. It functions almost like the sequel that was never made, expanding fans' experience of the pic. 'It's absolutely to build the franchises, to extend the franchises,' Wilson says. 'Consumers don't want a rehash of a movie.'" "Building franchises" becomes an open-ended process indeed. See David Bloom, "Viv U Finetunes Its Playbook," *Variety* (20–26 May 2002): 24.

27. See Henry Jenkins, *Textual Poachers: Television Fans & Participatory Culture* (New York: Routledge, 1992), especially chapter 6, "'Welcome to Bisexuality, Captain Kirk': Slash and the Fan-Writing Community," pp. 152–222. Essays on the "Batman" saga across many media and on its

fan culture appear in Roberta A. Pearson and William Uricchio, eds., *The Many Lives of the Batman* (New York: Routledge, 1991).

28. Recently, a parody of *Gone with the Wind*, *The Wind Done Gone* (2001), has been published; it too shows the original action from the point of view of a maid.

29. Conversely, in some cases the same artist may rework a single narrative, as in the recent phenomenon of the "director's cut." The director's cut of *The Exorcist* (William Friedkin, originally 1973) was released in 2000 and was surprisingly successful at the box office. *Apocalypse Now* (originally released in 1979) played at the 2001 Cannes Film Festival and then in general release with fifty-three minutes of unseen footage edited in by Francis Ford Coppola. DVDs frequently offer alternative versions and deleted scenes that are not part of the original but not exactly not part of the video version. Michael Mann's *Manhunter* (1986) was released on DVD with both the theatrical and director's versions, which differed by only three minutes. Steven Spielberg not only released a "Special Edition" of *Close Encounters of the Third Kind* (original 1977, "Special Edition" 1980) in theaters but re-edited the film into a third version for the 2001 DVD release. In 2002, New Line released two boxed DVD sets of *The Lord of the Rings: The Fellowship of the Ring*, one with the version released in theaters and a second with a "Special Extended Edition" containing about thirty extra minutes. Director Peter Jackson refused to call the latter a "director's cut," declaring himself to have been pleased with the film as edited and released (despite the fact that the film's theatrical trailers contained shots not in the film but restored to the special edition). By this point we can assume that directors of potential blockbusters keep in mind the DVD "director's cut" option even during the filming and editing stages for the theatrical version.

As in the case of old film libraries, we now see the phenomenon of recent footage gaining a new value when marketed in rereleases and video. Once again the idea of fixed narrative closure becomes fuzzy.

30. Victorian novels were issued in installments from the mid-1830s to the 1870s. At that point serial fiction of a respectable sort began appearing in English middle-class magazines, while "elongated penny dreadfuls" appeared in cheap newspapers. In this fashion, G. W. M. Reynolds's *Mysteries of London* and its sequel, *Mysteries in the Court of London*, ran for eleven years. For a succinct summary of these trends in England, see Richard D. Altick, "The Curse of the Cliffhanger," *Times*

Literary Supplement (9 February 2001): 5–6; for an overview of the middle-class British and American markets in magazine fiction during the late nineteenth and early twentieth centuries, see my *Wooster Proposes, Jeeves Disposes, or Le Mot Juste* (New York: James Heineman, 1992), pp. 22–25.

31. Some comic strips have continued as serials, but generally the self-contained gag has become the dominant norm. Similarly some comic books appear as serials; some even come out in a planned number of issues with closure, a sort of "miniseries" approach. (Indeed, it was recently announced that *Buffy*'s creator, Joss Whedon, will write an eight-issue "miniseries" comic-book story, not based on *Buffy*. See "Winner of the Week: Joss Whedon," *Entertainment Weekly* [18 May 2001]: 75.) These media are relatively insignificant, however, in comparison with the dominance of television.

32. Certainly the success of *The Lord of the Rings: The Fellowship of the Ring* (2001), combined with that of another initial installment in a serial, *Harry Potter and the Sorcerer's Stone* (2001), had a swift impact on approaches to creating "franchises." Companies began searching for promising family-oriented fantasy series for adaptation. In early 2002, within a few months of *Fellowship*'s release, New Line, the film's producer, bought the rights to Phillip Pullman's three-part *His Dark Materials*, comprised of *The Golden Compass* (1996), *The Subtle Knife* (1997), and *The Amber Spyglass* (2000).

A recent parallel trend, stemming from the popularity of the "Superman" and "Batman" films, has been the adaptation of comic books, a form that obviously encourages series. The huge success of *Spider-Man* (2002) can only accelerate this trend. See Tom Russo, "Monster Ink," *Entertainment Weekly* (10 May 2002): 38–45. On the sudden success of Marvel Entertainment's film-production division, Marvel Studios, see Ann Donahue, "Turnabout? It's Marvel-ous," *Variety* (20–26 May 2002): 6, 71.

4. THE STRANGE CASES OF DAVID LYNCH

1. Troy Patterson and Jeff Jensen, "Our Town," *Entertainment Weekly* 10th Anniversary Issue (Spring 2000): 101.

2. *Crouching Tiger* went on to win four Oscars and to earn over $200 million internationally.

3. David Bordwell, "The Art Cinema as a Mode of Film Practice," *Film Criticism* 4, no. 1 (1979): 57–61.

4. *Singing Detective* author Dennis Potter has recalled his dissatisfaction with Hollywood narrative based on his experience working for MGM on the film script of *Pennies from Heaven:* "When I was working in Hollywood I realised that the studio based all narrative forms entirely upon category. At the beginning of a project they would ask what particular bag it was in. Was it a detective story? Was it a musical? Was it a romance? They saw it as a marketing problem, even before the first shot. That sort of thinking throws a terrible carapace over the writer and one of the things I want to do in *The Singing Detective* is break up the narrative tyranny." Quoted from a 1986 *Radio Times* piece in Joost Hunningher, "*The Singing Detective,*" in George W. Brandt, ed., *British Television Drama in the 1980s* (Cambridge: Cambridge University Press, 1993), p. 240.

5. Potter has called the series a "pilgrimage": "*The Singing Detective* was not bleak, in my opinion, in that it attempted to show accurately what it is like to be stripped of everything and then to attempt, via cheap fiction and a mix of memory—distorted memory, invented memory and real memory—to reassemble oneself. It was, in itself, a pilgrimage, an act of optimism that began with total nihilistic despair and ended with someone walking out into the world." See Graham Fuller, ed., *Potter on Potter* (London: Faber and Faber, 1993), p. 91.

6. Bordwell, "The Art Cinema," p. 59.

7. Television is often said to be a producer's medium, but I am speaking strictly in terms of the creative side of television making. Moreover, frequently the head writer also serves as producer, which strengthens his or her control of the program: "'Television writers tell directors what to do,' explains *Everybody Loves Raymond* executive producer Phil Rosenthal. 'In television, the writer is king.' (Or at least executive producer, which is what TV writers are called when they get promoted.)" (Benjamin Svetkey, "Writer's Blockade," *Entertainment Weekly* [16 February 2001]: 27.) Moreover, most series rotate directors, so one director's distinctive style in his or her episodes would work against unity in the series as a whole.

8. See Fuller, ed., *Potter on Potter*, pp. 95–96.

9. Quoted in Kenneth C. Kaleta, *David Lynch* (New York: Twayne, 1993), p. 112.

10. Quoted in Paul A. Woods, *Weirdsville: The Obsessive Universe of David Lynch* (London: Plexus, 1997), p. 83.

11. Chris Rodley, ed., *Lynch on Lynch* (London: Faber and Faber, 1997), p. 168.

12. At least one analyst has interpreted *Twin Peaks* in a largely nonironic way that seems to echo Lynch's own sense of the "beauty" of the small-town life depicted here and in *Blue Velvet*. Tim Lucas takes the series to refer implicitly to the America of the 1950s: "When *Twin Peaks* touches on the '50s, it is only as we who remember them still feel them, as a vaguely golden loss. Its nostalgic metaphors are entwined with our contemporary national psychology: as a town and society, *Twin Peaks* is that virtual anachronism where the majesty of nature still abounds and simple pleasures like coffee and donuts are not merely commonplace but precious opportunities for communion with one's spirit." Tim Lucas, "Blood 'n Doughnuts," *Video Watchdog* 2 (1990): 35.

13. We should also note that, although the rock-throwing segment contains moments of humor, it yields fairly accurate results. Leo Johnson does turn out to have been one of the participants in the sordid events leading up to Laura's death, though he is not the actual murderer. A thrown rock also misses widely when Truman reads the name of Johnny Horne, a character completely uninvolved in the crime. The divination-by-rock-throwing also fits in with the supernatural elements that soon start creeping into the series, which include revelatory dreams and visions.

14. Woods, *Weirdsville*, p. 99.

15. Jean Rouverol, *Writing for Daytime Drama* (Boston: Focal Press, 1992), p. 300.

16. "It succeeds because it encompasses all television: soap opera, melodrama, murder mystery, situation comedy, high-school romance— *Twin Peaks* is the unabridged collection of television clichés." John Alexander, *The Films of David Lynch* (London: Charles Letts, 1993), p. 149.

17. Patterson and Jensen, "Our Town," p. 107.

18. Ibid., p. 96. Frost has also commented, "When David and I were working on *Twin Peaks*, our disagreements would mostly revolve around the fact that I wished for more clarity and David wanted to draw things out a little bit more—I mean, I think if David had had his way, we might *still* not know who killed Laura Palmer." Quoted in Woods, *Weirdsville*, p. 140.

Lynch comments in more detail on his desire to delay the revelation in an interview with Chris Rodley, editor of *Lynch on Lynch:*

"[Rodley:] By the time we get to the answer—that it was Leland— it doesn't really seem to matter any more. By then it's clear that an evil force—Bob—is operating from within the 'host' character anyway. So pointing the finger at Leland isn't really an answer at all.

"[Lynch:] It's not an answer. That was the whole point. Mark Frost and I had this idea. The way we pitched this thing was as a murder mystery but that murder mystery was to eventually become the background story. Then there would be a middle ground of all the characters we stay with for the series. And the foreground would be the main characters that particular week: the ones we'd deal with in detail. We're not going to solve the murder for a long time.

"This they did *not* like. They did *not* like that. And they forced us to, you know, get to Laura's killer. It wasn't really all their fault. People just got a bug in them that they wanted to know who killed Laura Palmer. Calling out for it. And one thing led to another, and the pressure was just so great that the murder mystery couldn't be just a background thing anymore. The progress towards it, but never getting there, was what made us *know* all the people in Twin Peaks: how they all surrounded Laura and intermingled. All the mysteries. But it wasn't meant to be. It just couldn't happen that way. The yearning to know was too intense. But the mystery was the magical ingredient. It would've make *Twin Peaks* live a lot longer.

"[Rodley:] On the other hand, that intense desire on the audience's behalf to find the answer to the mystery testifies to the impact of the series.

"[Lynch:] Yeah but, you know, it killed the thing.

"[Rodley:] So, in your original plan, the unmasking of Leland would have been much later?

"[Lynch:] Way, way later. And who knows how it would've unfolded then? But there'd be a yearning—maybe subconscious—to know. It's the same thing with *The Fugitive* [the TV series]: where is that one-armed man? Yet each week, you know, they hardly ever dealt with that. And that's the beautiful thing. You keep wondering, 'When will he find this guy and set everything straight?' But then you knew that would be the end.

"[Rodley:] But it made perfect sense, as the real killer was not flesh and blood, that the story could continue—almost for ever. It defies resolution. I sort of assume that *Twin Peaks* is still there, it's just that no one is pointing the camera at it now.

"[Lynch:] Right. That's a good way to think. I know that world and I love it so much. It's a real pull to go back and revisit it. Bob was one part of *Twin Peaks* that could've lived on and been dealt with in different ways."

Rodley, *Lynch on Lynch*, pp. 180-181.

19. Frost has remarked of *Hill Street Blues*: "*Hill Street* was very good, but it was very impersonal work for me. I wrote about that place as if I was a visitor. It wasn't what my life was like. It was a great place to learn the craft of how to shape a scene, but I wanted a chance to write about more personal themes and obsessions. My point of view has always been more offbeat." Thus in *Twin Peaks* Frost combined his network training with an odd sensibility that enabled him to work with his far odder collaborator.

For Frost's remarks about *Hill Street Blues* and more on the connections between *Twin Peaks* and *Hill Street Blues*, see Tom Stempel, *Storytellers to the Nation: A History of American Television Writing* (New York: Continuum, 1992), p. 244.

20. Rodley, *Lynch on Lynch*, p. 162. Asked by the same interviewer to describe the pitch session that sold *Twin Peaks* to ABC, Lynch makes it sound like a conventional *Hill Street Blues*–style narrative: "The mystery of who killed Laura Palmer was the foreground, but this would recede slightly as you go to know the other people in the town and the problems they were having. And each week would feature close-ups of some things. The project was to mix a police investigation with the ordinary lives of the characters" (p. 158). Any ABC executive who recalled such a pitch must have been startled to see the Red Room dream scene, the plotlines involving the Black Lodge, mysterious signals from outer space, and all the rest of the supernatural developments that began quite early on.

Lynch has also described how the process of spinning out new narrative material from the basic plot arc resulted in the series' most notoriously experimental sequence. Under their contract with ABC, Lynch and Frost were required to make a separate version of their two-hour pilot for European theatrical release. In the eighteen-minute final portion shot specifically for the European version, the mystery of Laura Palmer's murder had to be solved. Predictably, Lynch thought that such an ending was "absurd," but he helped shoot and edit it. During the editing process, "this thing popped into my head about the Red Room . . . It led to another layer of what would be *Twin Peaks*. Having to do a closed ending opened up a [creative path] that would never have happened. Sometimes being forced into a corner is not a bad thing" (Patterson and Jensen, "Our Town," p. 101). The Red Room scene was used in Episode 3 of the first ABC series (the same one with the Tibet sequence), opening up the Bob motif and all the dream material relating to the Man from Another World, the Giant, and the general supernatural theme that became more prominent in the second season. Thus Lynch managed to seize on the restrictions imposed on him by his contract to generate ever-expanding plot material.

21. Marc Dolan has written an idiosyncratic analysis of seriality in *Twin Peaks*, arguing that the series lost its audience because, in the first season, it followed the conventions of an episodic serial (i.e., a murder to be solved), and in the second it took a new direction and became an open-ended, multiple-story soap opera. Dolan considers this switch a collective miscalculation on the part of Frost, Lynch, and ABC executives, who threw away a chance to build a loyal audience of the type *Dallas* and *Dynasty* had. He argues that the first season was ill-conceived, while the second went in a more promising direction—an opinion that runs counter to most others concerning the relative quality of the two seasons. This take also assumes that Lynch somehow was concerned to build a hit for ABC, while it is apparent that he simply wanted to play with the open-ended possibilities of the many characters for as long as he and Frost could manage to keep the series going. Given the huge amount of attention *Twin Peaks* attracted during its first season, they might well have believed that the run would be a long one.

See Marc Dolan, "Peaks and Valleys of Serial Creativity," in David Lavery, ed., *Full of Secrets: Critical Approaches to Twin Peaks* (Detroit: Wayne State University Press, 1995), pp. 30–50.

22. Woods, *Weirdsville*, p. 96.

23. As critics Michelle Le Blanc and Colin Odell point out, this rapid-fire summary comes, not at the beginning of the second-season premiere, but as a follow-up to a more-than-leisurely opening scene: "Lynch opened season two with a feature length episode that was alienating, frustrating and brilliant. Instead of instant resolution of any of the multitude of cliffhangers, he produced twelve interminable minutes of Cooper, wounded and immobile from his gunshot wound, negotiating a glass of

milk with a geriatric waiter and receiving cryptic riddles from a Scandinavian giant. In retrospect, this is a wonderfully restrained piece of comedy that rewards with each subsequent visit, but on first viewing it is excruciating in the extreme. Once discovered, Cooper is rushed to hospital and the current predicaments of all the major characters are reeled off by Lucy in about 30 seconds!" Michelle Le Blanc and Colin Odell, *David Lynch* (Harpenden, Herts.: Pocket Essentials, 2000), p. 50.

Tim Lucas was disappointed with the first-series finale, finding it lamentably clichéd. In doing so he unintentionally points up another of the series' parodic devices: "The cliffhanger capped nine of the wittiest and most challenging hours ever televised with a storyline so bereft of originality that it actually left damsels in distress in a burning saw mill." Lucas, "Blood 'n Doughnuts," p. 34.

24. I might add that, although I chose my examples from memory without looking up where they came in the series, they all turned out to be from episodes directed by Lynch.

25. See "Checklist of Twin Peaks Magazine Articles," *Wrapped in Plastic* 1 (October 1992): 14–16; and "Checklist of Twin Peaks Magazine Articles, part 2," *Wrapped in Plastic* 2 (December 1992): 14–18.

26. The box of the Granada Media video release of the series' first season contains a revealing set of quotations:

"By some distance the bleakest and best new British sitcom of the year" *(Guardian)*.

"Poignant, funny, inventive and beautifully written . . . a masterpiece" *(Daily Mail)*.

"The best sitcom of the decade" *(Time Out)*.

"A complete waste of my licence fee" *(a bald London cabbie)*.

Although the series itself deals with a working-class family, the quotations, taken together, suggest that the video promoters perceived *The Royle Family*'s primary audience to be intellectuals, who don't mind a bit of bleakness in the service of art. The quotations seem more likely to insult than attract potential working-class purchasers.

In fact, working-class audiences like *The Royle Family* very much. Not only have the video releases been best-sellers in Britain, but cheekily vulgar posters featuring the characters have been available in the local Virgin Megatore in Oxford. Intellectuals with whom I discussed the series seemed adamantly divided over whether it was brilliant or beneath notice.

The producers seem to have belatedly realized that *The Royle Fam-*

ily had a considerable working-class following. The blurbs on the back of the second-season video release came from sources more likely to appeal to this group:

"It's a right Royle treat!" *(The Sun).*

"No family could be that foul—or that funny" *(The Mirror).*

"The real Royle family—accept no imitations" *(The Express).*

27. Even when characters look out the windows and comment on what is going on outside, we are never given their point of view on that action. The real-time dramaturgy of *The Royle Family*'s episodes goes against the tendency of short-form programs to be broken up into balanced large-scale parts.

28. The second season of *The Royle Family* introduced more potentially important causal actions that came to nothing. Anthony mentions at the end of one episode that he is managing a rock band and asks brother-in-law Craig to get them a gig at a bar where he works; at the beginning of the next episode the family asks how the rock band is doing, and he says that it has broken up. (A similar action occurs in the third season, when the band is revived in one episode, not to be mentioned again.) Barbara's advancing menopause provides a motif as she becomes irritable and annoyed with Jim; in Episode 5 it seems to create a crisis as Barbara stalks out of the house. (During the quarrel among Denise, Craig, and Jim that follows, Jim mentions that Barbara does not always provide his "tea" on time because of her job in the bakery—a brief reference to the dangling cause set up in Episode 1 of the first season.) But Barbara soon returns, saying she had just gone for a walk; Jim quietly tells her that they'll get through her "change" together. Once again seemingly important dramatic conflicts are short-lived (and Barbara's menopause is never mentioned in the seven episodes of the third season). The season ends as Jim, in a rare display of charm, offers to make tea and even dinner the next night. Denise's pregnancy gives a sense of how much time passes during the second season, but the baby is born in the gap between the second and third seasons.

It may be worth noting that *The Royle Family*, like *Fawlty Towers*, is scripted and coproduced by two of its main actors, Caroline Aherne (who plays Denise) and Craig Cash (Dave).

29. In a critique of recent British art, critic and historian Julian Stallabrass has offered a telling comparison of *The Simpsons* to what he calls "high art lite," that is, recent gallery art aimed at entertaining an elite class of consumers: "To hold up *The Simpsons* against this art is in-

structive, for it very successfully does what high art lite is supposed to do—appeals to different viewers on a number of levels. Its consistently critical message is delivered to huge audiences, the references being complex, knowing and piled on at huge speed. It has many of the qualities of high art lite without the signal disadvantage of being high art. As with high art lite, the spectacle of degradation it presents is an entertaining one. Yet *The Simpsons'* critique is radical because it implies that fallibility and corruption are not just a matter of individuals but of systems, and it offers some small and faintly glimpsed positive elements to set against the dystopian vision, particularly in the feelings of the main characters for each other. The challenge such a programme offers to high art lite is the following: is there anything that it does that art can do better (other than sell unique objects to millionaires)?" Julian Stallabrass, *High Art Lite* (London/New York: Verso, 1999), p. 168.

30. Matt Groening, Ray Richmond, and Antonia Coffman, *The Simpsons: A Complete Guide to Our Favorite Family* (New York: HarperCollins, 1997); Matt Groening and Scott M. Gimple, *The Simpsons Forever! A Complete Guide to Our Favorite Family . . . Continued* (New York: HarperCollins, 1999); and Jesse L. McCann, ed., *The Simpsons Beyond Forever! A Complete Guide to Our Favorite Family . . . Still Continued* (New York: HarperCollins, 2002).

31. Homer's inconsistent traits are clearly of great use in generating plots. He ranges from fairly clever to grotesquely dense, and the scriptwriters flaunt the impossible contrasts shamelessly. For example, in "Kidney Trouble" (6 December 1998), the following exchange occurs as Homer is about to drive home with his family, including his elderly father:

Grandpa: "Can I go to the bathroom before we leave?"

Homer: "But we gotta get home. I don't want to miss *Inside the Actors' Studio.* Tonight is F. Murray Abraham."

Grandpa: "But I really need to—"

Homer, emphatically: "F. Murray Abraham!"

Most jokes involve Homer's ignorance and anti-intellectualism, but here for no particular reason the writers motivate his refusal to allow his father to visit a rest room in this way.

A similar case occurs in "Lady Bouvier's Lover" (12 May 1994), in which, for reasons we need not examine here, Bart hands Homer $350 in cash. Homer reacts ecstatically: "$350! Now I can buy 70 transcripts of *Nightline!*" Other characters occasionally behave in surprising ways, but none comes anywhere near the extremes of Homer's traits. Given that character consistency is one of the mainstays of classical narrative, Homer provides one of the main reasons that one could argue for at least some episodes of *The Simpsons* being art television.

32. The creators of *The Simpsons* are well aware that their audience includes intellectuals. The series' many film and television allusions include "art" items, such as "22 Short Films about Springfield" (14 April 1996), derived from the documentary *Thirty-Two Short Films about Glenn Gould* (1993). Two episodes refer to *Twin Peaks:* the classic "Who Shot Mr. Burns? (Part Two)" premiere of the 1995–96 season featured a parody of the backward-talking Red-Room dream, and the "Lisa's Sax" episode (19 October 1997) showed Homer totally absorbed in watching *Twin Peaks,* then muttering as he pretends to enjoy its irony: "Brilliant—heh, heh, heh. I have absolutely no idea what's going on." In April 2001, *The Simpsons* presented an elaborate parody of Tom Tykwer's German art film, *Run Lola Run* (1999). An indication of the series' range of references came in the two successive episodes of 11 April and 25 April 1999, the guest voices for which were, respectively, Jasper Johns and Jack La Lanne.

33. Rupert Murdoch has appeared on *The Simpsons.* In "Sunday, Cruddy Sunday" (31 January 1999), Homer goes to the Superbowl and accidently invades Murdoch's skybox. Its owner appears and angrily introduces himself to Homer: "I'm Rupert Murdoch, the billionaire tyrant, and this is my skybox." Lest it be thought that the creative team were clandestinely biting the hand that feeds them, it should be noted that Murdoch provided his own voice for this scene.

34. This episode, "Marge Simpson in: 'Screaming Yellow Honkers,'" aired 21 February 1999.

INDEX